WHY HIRE YOU?

Dayna Williams

Bethany Mangin

ISBN: 0615809111
ISBN 13: 9780615809113

Library of Congress Control Number: 2013939837
Strong Tower Press, Philadelphia, PA

TABLE OF CONTENTS

INTRODUCTION

We can all agree—it's rough out there! If you have spent any time looking for employment, changing careers, or reentering the workforce, you know how hard it is just to get a phone call, let alone an interview and job offer. So we are glad that you found us! We are two working human resource executives with a combined twenty years of experience who have assembled a large network of other HR professionals who make hiring decisions every day. We know from our own experience and from talking with others that it's not uncommon to get two hundred resumes within a matter of a few days for the positions that we post. Then, after we somehow manage to narrow down that list and call candidates in, quite often they are unprepared or cannot set themselves apart from the other five people we are interviewing. So, you might ask, "What are you looking for when you are hiring?" Good question!

We are simply looking for the answer to the question, *Why You*? Remember, if you get the opportunity to interview, it is because someone in the company thinks you are qualified to be sitting across the table. However, it does not stop there; the interview is yours to win or lose. If you really want the position, then you as the candidate need to seal the deal and articulate exactly why someone should choose you. This is simple in theory but not so much in practice. Ever try to paint a picture for someone as to what you bring to the table in just a few sentences so that it *really* sticks?

If you have tried this before, you have probably found it is not as easy as it seems. It can be hard to summarize years of education, skills, or experience into a few high-impact statements. If you have not tried this before, then you should. Hiring managers are busy people! They have stacks of resumes of qualified candidates who all want the same thing that you do. And those hiring managers have their own job responsibilities, bosses, and lives outside of work, just like you. There is so much competing for their time and attention.

The challenge is that most books and resources out there, although well-intentioned, won't focus on the reality of the hiring manager's day-to-day responsibilities or point of view—at least at first. They'll talk about how to write a great resume or which interview questions to expect. That's fantastic, but what if twenty other people who all applied for the same job that you did read those same books and resources? What if all twenty of you showed up with great resumes and experience, wearing snazzy suits, and prepared to answer the same top interview questions? If you were a hiring manager, who would *you* hire?

As people who make hiring decisions every day and who advise others to make good hiring decisions, let us answer that question for you. All things being equal, hiring managers will look at the choices in front of them and select the person who can clearly communicate how he or she will do the job best. In short, they choose candidates who can answer the question that everyone wants to know—*why* hire them over the other guys? Hiring managers operate in this mindset because quite often their jobs are on the line, and they are accountable for the decisions they make and the people they bring into the organization.

In this book, we will introduce you to a simple, three-step approach that you can use to start training yourself to think,

Why You? This way of thinking will power the way that you assess what you bring to the table, plan your job search, write your resumes and cover letters, and present yourself in an interview so that you stand apart from whoever else wants that job.

Now, we assume a few things of you, the reader, as you work through the concepts in this book. First, we assume that you have some version of a resume and cover letter that you developed, perhaps as part of a college career class. Of course, if you are a working professional, then you have a resume and cover letter somewhere in your files. If you don't have a resume and cover letter yet, there are plenty of templates and great resources that will help you develop a draft at the very least. Then we'll help you take that draft from good to great in this book. Second, we assume that you have some sense of the field, industry, and position that you would like to get hired into. If you do not have a direction or are still exploring your options, then there are resources you can find online that will help acquaint you with various career paths and jobs based on your personality, interests, and abilities. In this book, we will help turn your current career direction into an actionable plan that ensures your happiness and success.

As you read through, you will see that we focus on the "need to know" information that will make a significant difference in the way that you approach your job search and how you interview. We will provide examples and resources so that you can apply the concepts to your own real-life situations. We don't promise to cover everything related to the enormous topic of careers, but we will get straight to the point of what is most important to take your game to the next level, because we know that in some cases you need a job now! And if you are going to make your best effort to get that job, then you will have to do some key things right along the way. At the core of what you will learn here is *a new way of thinking*, and you will be able to apply this new way of thinking to planning your career, setting goals, fine-tuning your job search, and exceptional interviewing. We also invite you to apply these *Why Hire You* techniques the next time that you have your eye on a promotion! So come journey with us as we provide you with exactly what you need to get to where you want to go.

WHY: THE A³ MODEL

Simple Principle: You are busy. Employers are busier. You need a simple strategy that you can use to assess how you can best connect the dots between what you bring and what companies need so that you can get hired over other candidates.

Morning, Sam! I just learned that the head of a critical business unit just resigned, so we have to fill that slot ASAP. Also, we lost the budget to use outside recruiters, which means our team will have to double up and start recruiting ourselves. For compliance purposes, we will need to thoroughly document all of our interviews, even though that is additional work on your plate. I think your 9:00 a.m. interview just arrived and is in the lobby.

Organizations and the people who work for them are busy! On any given day, they have to meet customer service demands, create new products, manage their numbers, and plan for their futures. They know that much of that success depends on having the *right* people in the *right* positions. However, everyone is time crunched, and it is not uncommon in this economy for people to be wearing several different hats within a company. So, while you may have a great set of skills and experience, consider our opening example. Sam is a human resource manager who has a lot going on, and her boss is piling more responsibilities on her plate. Now, imagine that you are the 9:00 a.m. candidate waiting to be interviewed. The pressure is on *you* to stand out. If you show up in Sam's office like most people do—typically ready to talk about themselves in generalities—then in a matter of about ten minutes or so, Sam will probably scribble a few notes down and then start drifting off to think about the new executive who has to be hired and how much harder her job just got overnight now that she will have extra responsibilities. It is important to realize that you are not just competing against other people for a job; you are competing against a whole variety of things going on behind the scenes. For that reason, you must bring your game up to the next level.

Let's dial it back, for a moment, to the point in time before we even get to the interview phase. Although there are more and more jobs becoming available every day, we can still acknowledge that for the time being, especially for newer college grads, we are still in an "employers' market." So when a hiring manager has a job opportunity posted, they are deluged with resumes—at times even hundreds—from people who want the same position. Can you picture this for a moment? What would you do if you were a manager with full-time responsibilities and a job opening on your team, yet you received dozens of good candidates for this one position? Would you carefully investigate each one, overlook errors, or forgive vague statements? What about mixed messages or resumes that are mismatched for the position? Remember Sam's situation. What do you think she would do now that she has to be an HR manager and a recruiter, essentially doing two full-time jobs in one forty-hour week? The reality is that hiring managers don't have time to sift through your back story to see if it makes sense or connect the dots between your skills and what is required for the role. They need *you* to make the strong case for *them*. From our experience, very few people do this well.

By the time you are done with this book, we want you to understand why it is important to be clear about what you bring to the table and how to be one of the few people who can connect the dots for hiring managers by making that case. You will do this by developing and using a strong set of tools (cover letter, resume) and then, of course, by acing the interview. We want you to gain and sustain the advantage. The essence of this approach can be summarized by three simple words: Why Hire You. If you find along the way that you have gaps in your skills or experience that you need to plug, we will provide suggestions for next steps that you can take.

Now that we have talked about the importance behind the Why Hire You (**WHY** for short) approach, we will introduce you to a simple, repeatable process called the A³ model. This model is the power behind the WHY approach, and it helps you fully assess your current situation to determine what you bring to the table and how to connect what you bring with what employers need and want. The A³ model has three easy steps:

- **Assess** who you are, what you want, and what skills you bring

- **Absorb** professional insights that will turn who you are into what companies need

- **Articulate** why an employer should hire you by easily connecting the dots between who you are, what you bring, and how that meets company needs

A³Model

Assess

Absorb

Articulate

- **Assess** Yourself Professionally

- **Absorb** Professional Insights

- **Articulate** your W.H.Y.

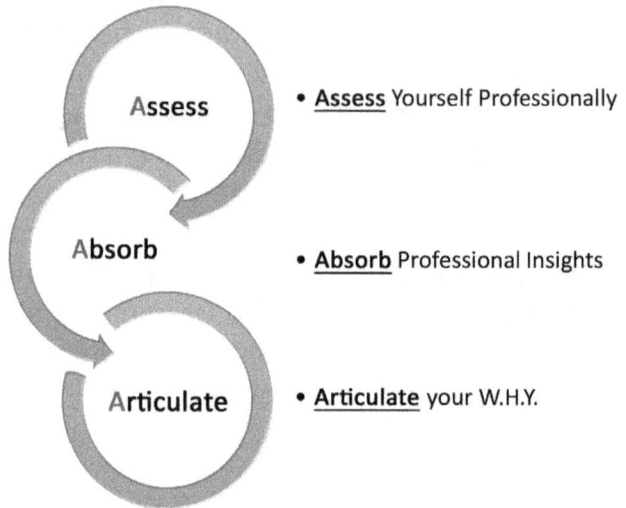

The A³ model brings structure to the WHY approach to make it actionable. It works for you by enabling you to put a plan in motion, whether you are setting goals, evaluating jobs, or preparing for an interview, and makes hiring managers happy by saving them valuable time in the interviewing process. They finally have a candidate who can paint the picture for them of what it will be like if they get hired into the job that they need to fill.

Bottom Line: The A³ model brings structure to the WHY approach to make it actionable. The simple, three-step process of **Assess, Absorb,** and **Articulate** helps you to determine what you bring to the table and connect it to what employers need and want so you can get hired.

THE HAPPINESS FACTOR

Simple Principle: Your personal happiness matters. Successful people who love what they do and grow in their careers take the time to visualize where they are now and where they want to go in the future. Then they plan the necessary steps to make that happen instead of leaving it to chance.

To a hiring manager, every standout resume tells a story, a story that easily conveys a Why Hire You message. These resumes should show that the candidate has had a clearly defined path and has been successful in his or her career decisions. He or she is a dedicated, happy individual who possesses valuable skills coveted by every employer. Don't we all want to be that person?

Before we begin to unpack the A^3 model, we should say that we know that some new college grads who are a little light in their skills and experience, as well as some successful professionals who have been caught in the realities of this job market, are not yet ready to rush ahead with **Assess**. So if that is you, we are going to help shape your thinking as you browse the job boards and speak with your family and friends about opportunities. If you do know where you are headed and are ready to proceed full steam ahead with **Assess**, then you may wish to skip ahead to the next chapter. Or perhaps you, too, will pause and continue with us for a few more pages so that you can use the following information as a quick validation that you are indeed firmly planted on a path that will bring you continued professional and personal happiness. This is important because, as we will show you, your professional and personal happiness will heavily impact your life for the next five, ten, or twenty-some years.

We begin with a simple truth: *Your personal happiness matters.* Bet that made you smile—we saw it! At the risk of sounding self-indulgent, consider recent research that suggests that less than half of working Americans report being happy with their jobs, and only an estimated 20 percent of people are satisfied with their careers. Because you will spend approximately 73,000 hours of your adult life at work, it is clear why securing an insurance policy for your professional happiness is critical.

If we draw on some of our own personal experiences as a blueprint for advising you on how to look at your personal situation, we can honestly say that although we have had some good opportunities come our way, in most cases we have intentionally put ourselves in positions to make things happen. Ask yourself this question: If you were to interview for your dream opportunity tomorrow morning, what exciting things would set you apart from twenty other people that the interviewer would be meeting? What would you talk about? Responsibilities at your current job waiting tables? Good, but perhaps not entirely relevant. Your personal interests? Not appropriate. Your creativity or intellect? Too subjective.

We want you to be ready to shine for when that dream opportunity arises. To prepare for that inevitable moment, you have to begin with an honest assessment of where you are right now. Whether you are still in college deciding on a major, contemplating graduate school, or looking to make a career change, do not take another significant step until you can define what professional happiness and success means to you. You need to have this snapshot of yourself so that you can determine the right path to pursue and start building or expanding that standout resume that will show a hiring manager that you are well into building a stable career that is professionally enriching and makes you happy.

By taking some time to define your personal happiness now, you allow yourself to make career-based decisions that will best position you to achieve personal happiness at each and every stage in your professional life—an accomplishment that is impossible to achieve without some level of planning. Let us give you some things to think about as you define your personal happiness.

Does Happiness Mean...	YES	NO
Working a set schedule M-F, 9:00-5:00?		
Working indoors in the same environment all day long?		
Traveling two-to-three weeks out of the month and perhaps working from home?		
Regularly interacting with people all day long?		
Being task-oriented and interacting with a few people each day?		
Commuting longer than 30 minutes each way?		
Working in a large company where you get lost in the crowd?		
Being a part of a small company where you do five jobs for the pay of one?		
Pursuing a career that gives you flexibility to start and stop for family reasons?		
Working around the clock for the first 10-15 years so that you can semi-retire comfortably later on?		
Choosing a field that is not your first choice because it is financially lucrative?		
Making the most money possible?		
Making a genuine contribution to society?		
Paying your dues at the bottom for a while until you can work your way to the top?		
Managing other people and working through the challenges of individual personalities?		
Having multiple careers throughout your lifetime to keep your life fresh and challenging?		
Being highly visible in your profession and acknowledged for your achievements?		

For most people it is not natural to ask themselves all these questions, but it is critical that you understand what it is that makes you tick as a person. Here is some advice: think beyond what happiness means to you *today* and consider what some of your personal and professional aspirations are, both short-term and several years out. Why is this crucial? Because there is no question that life changes, and often a career that makes someone happy now can become a real drag as he or she progresses through life. When people do not make some effort to plan ahead, they find themselves confronting life changes and making reactive, instead of proactive, career decisions. For example, a reactive career decision looks something like this:

> *Sarah began a career track by holding positions within a financial company, each with increasing responsibility. After a few years, she learned that her boss wanted to promote her; however, she would need to earn a Series 7 certification in order to obtain that promotion. The certification would require many extra hours dedicated to studying, something that Sarah did not want to do at that point in her life. If she stayed in her current position, she risked her boss seeing her as an underperformer, and she would likely never get another promotion. So Sarah reacted to this situation by taking a position in sales, because it was the only position she could get that paid her a similar salary. However, one year into the sales job, Sarah wanted out. She did not like the pressure of monthly goals and the long hours. Her resume left potential hiring managers with the impression that she had an uncertain professional identity.*

This is an example of what happens to many people who have to make major career transitions for reasons such as not wanting to pursue an advanced degree or certification, lack of upward mobility in their chosen field, or just plain boredom. These people find themselves in the unfortunate position of having to start at the bottom again. And remember: A job change may seem right for today, but a resume is forever. When you bounce all over the place because a job seems like a good or better opportunity, that decision is memorialized each time on the big picture snapshot of your career that is your resume. One such job move may be explainable, but several over the course of three, five, or ten years shows a potential hiring manager that you do not know what makes you happy or tick as a professional. They may disregard you as a candidate for fear that you too will leave them for the next great opportunity. We see this happen every day. Resumes come across our desks that don't make sense. They tell a story of people who will seemingly work anywhere instead of being intentional about pursuing internships or positions in the field that they really want to be in. So we are going to give our jobs to people who show us on a resume that they love what we do. If we are in the retail business, then we want to see that you have experience in our business! And not just as a cashier. Even if you are just out of college, we want to see that you took on a winter internship to support an inventory project or temped as a coordinator. That shows us you have skin in the game, so we are much more likely to take a chance on you.

Here is another common situation that often affects young college grads the most. Some find that they graduate college with a great level of passion and energy. These students leave the structure and routine of university life and may think that they are immediately ready to obtain a high-octane position in which they are traveling all over the globe meeting new people and seeing new places. This sounds exciting—the possibilities are endless! And why not travel on the company's dime? However, five or six years down the line, their life situations change, and all of sudden they begin looking for positions that keep them closer to home. Sometimes this works out, but many times they find it is not so easy to make the change because they have chosen a path that requires that they maintain that high-octane professional lifestyle if they desire to keep their income level. They begin to realize that sometimes changing jobs because of lifestyle needs may mean having to accept a lower salary. This can be very challenging if their personal expenses have risen to a certain level, perhaps because of purchasing a home or having children.

We just used travel as one example of something that may sound good when you are starting out or during one phase of your life, but needs to be fully assessed to determine whether it can impact your personal happiness down the line. So what do you do if you determine that you might like travel now, but you don't think you want to travel forever? You plan for it! You choose a path that gives you some freedom now with a deliberate plan for the future rather than just leaving it to chance. For example, maybe you will plan for a sales job that includes travel now, but put a plan in motion to move into an inside sales job within the next five years. You will start targeting particular companies locally that have large inside sales forces well in advance so that you can start meeting people and making connections at around the three-year mark. You get to know them; they get to know you. Your plan eventually works. Two years later, you are settled into your inside sales role and the days of travel are a distant yet colorful set of digital photos on your laptop.

You see, when taking the time to review what makes you happy, it is important to consider these smaller things like travel in addition to loftier goals, like salaries or titles that typically come to mind for most people. In our experience, the smaller things such as choosing the size of the company you work for, tend to impact happiness as much as those bigger goals. Let's say that you are three years out of school and have been employed with a small company of twenty-five people. You find yourself with multiple responsibilities: sales, office support, marketing. They name it; you do it. And in the process you work fifty hours a week for a forty-hour-per-week salary. Then you go to lunch with a friend you went to school with who is working for a large company and making 20 percent more than you are doing one job—and gym membership is a perk. You think to yourself that maybe you would be better suited for that type of environment. But you have three years under your belt, and you don't want to start at entry level. And for a position equivalent to the level you are at now, the large company gets hundreds of applicants and will only choose candidates with experience working in similarly sized firms. Determining what size company you want to work for and realizing how a company's size translates into its work environment and what that means for your everyday job matters.

Continuing with our example of company size, if you are the type of person who loves to be a "big fish in a small pond" and likes to have a lot of responsibility but only get paid for one job—people who work for small companies call this "wearing many hats," and they smile proudly when saying it—then perhaps working for a small company (one hundred people or fewer) is your cup of tea. However, if you like order, systems, processes, structures, resources, and departments in which everyone has one focus, place, and purpose in the organization, then a large company (5,000 or more people) is best for you. If you find yourself at a midsize company (101–5,000 people) you may be able to get some of the best qualities of both small and large companies; however, it is possible that you may also experience some of the "growing pains" that medium-sized businesses face as they strive to reach their next level of growth potential.

These are just a few examples of situations that people can find themselves in that can be totally avoided through some honest evaluation of how you define professional happiness. We suggest taking some time to think through what you have pictured so far for yourself in terms of next professional steps. Then go back and take some time to honestly read through the *Happiness Factor* questions again to carefully consider whether your decisions *today* will lead you down a path of professional and personal happiness tomorrow, five, and ten years from now.

Here is a little personal story. I (Dayna) once had an interview with a large global company in New York City. It was certain to be the position that would take my young career in marketing to the international stage and allow me to work alongside the best and the brightest. The interview process was going very well, and then the director of human resources informed me that working for the industry leader meant that I would have to be "global and mobile" and that the possibility of me landing in France at some point in the future was highly probable. After the interview on the plane flight back to Los Angeles, I could not get the words "global and mobile" out of my head. Back then, as a twenty-something-year-old without personal responsibilities such as family and kids, the prospect of being global and mobile sounded pretty darn exciting!

However, the more I reflected on what my personal life might be like two to five years down the road, I realized that being global and mobile might actually screw up or at least delay certain future goals that I had in my personal life. So, approximately five years into my career, I had *finally* learned not to jump at every opportunity that sounded exciting but rather to take a step back and think about where I wanted to be in two to five years. I realized from that point on that I needed to seek positions that would challenge me professionally and reward me financially but would also offer me the flexibility and convenience of being close to home and offer a good work/life balance. Sounds like a tall order, right? I knew that the time to start down that path was right then, at the five-year mark, so that down the road, instead of packing for Paris, my professional and personal life would be nicely aligned. I am happy to report today that as you read this book, several years later, I am a home-based executive working for a smaller, US-based company managing a team of learning professionals in a role requiring minimal travel, mostly at my discretion.

When engaging in career goal setting, first remind yourself of how you define happiness and success. Summarize your definition into a few key bullet points. Then ask yourself the following questions:

- What are my professional goals in three to five years?

- What are my short-term and long-term personal and/or family goals?

- What aspects of my professional life do I need to control in order to compliment my personal and/or family goals? (Think about travel, relocation, long hours, shifts, weekends, etc.)

- Do I envision one long, continuous career, or do I anticipate a career change? If I anticipate a career change, when?

- Do I plan on furthering my education at some point in my career? If so, when?

It is very reasonable for you to be thinking that you do not have all the answers to these questions right now, and that is OK. By pondering these questions, answering the ones that you can, and creating a basic framework of how you envision your life both professionally and personally, you are off to a good start. This effort will put you on the right path to achieving your personal happiness. You will be better off creating a framework of how you define happiness now and continue to revise it throughout your career as opposed to walking blindly into the future hoping that it will all just work itself out—because, of course, your happiness is too important to leave to chance.

Design Your Path

Now that you have considered your personal happiness, it's time to connect the dots and design your career path. Let's explore this concept using an illustration. We'll assume that in this scenario, a young woman named Amy wants to have a career in human resources, and in five years she wants to be a manager for a midsize firm where she will be responsible for a group of employees and earn a comfortable salary.

When designing a career path, it is always best to determine where you would like to be in five years and work backward by turning the skills, education, and requirements for that position into a career checklist for yourself. Using Amy's scenario, within the world of HR a typical career progression could look like beginning at a coordinator level, then moving into the role of generalist and finally being promoted to manager. If Amy were a coordinator today and were to pencil in that her five-year goal is to reach manager status, then as a reasonable three-year goal, Amy should be focusing on moving into a generalist position. The generalist level essentially has responsibility over many human resource functions providing someone like Amy with a range of experience. She could build upon that experience and start to develop her skills in a more specific area to position herself in a few years to become the manager that she aspires to be. As year one, year three, and year five goals are established, we can now see a career path taking shape that, when combined with a track record of solid performance, is continuously advancing upward and will lead directly to achieving professional success.

One of the best ways to get a glimpse into what your five-year plan might look like is to go to any online job board (CareerBuilder, Indeed, etc.) and, using the nationwide search function, type in the title of the position that you want to achieve in the next three or five years. For example, if you are right out of college, you might move out of an internship and into a full-time assistant role. Then you might move from there into a coordinator role like Amy.

If we conduct this search based on Amy's scenario, in which her five-year goal is to become a manager of human resources, then we might come across a job posting like this:

Z & R Company

Human Resources Manager

Job Summary:

An organization located in the US seeks a Human Resource Manager with ability to partner with various managers and their teams to develop and execute the HR strategies and planning activities to support our people.

Position Responsibilities:

- Ability to understand business priorities and translate them into an HR agenda that supports the business.
- Assess the human resources needs in areas such as performance management, employee relations, compensation, career development and leadership development.
- Diagnose problems as well as identify and drive appropriate solutions.
- Work with professionals at all levels of the organization.
- Possess excellent communication skills, coaching skills, strategic thinking and planning/project management skills, as well as the ability to thrive in a fast-paced environment.

Skills Required:

- Master's Degree preferred
- PHR Certification
- Experience in executive coaching
- Strategic thinking skills and ability to drive towards appropriate solutions
- Process improvement in people strategies and initiatives
- Strong project/program management skills
- Ability to relate to, influence and coach employees across the organization
- Effective communication skills - written, verbal and listening
- Ability to work independently as well as part of a business and HR team

---

This job description would give Amy a list of skills, experience, and education to aim for as she looks down the five-year road. She would pursue projects at work that would give her this type of experience, consider enrolling in a graduate program if she is really serious, and ensure that she earns the valuable Professional Human Resource (PHR) certification when appropriate. Having insight into what companies want enables Amy to do the right things along the way to make herself as marketable as possible for when the time comes to make a move.

You can repeat this same three- to five-year planning and goal-setting process throughout your career and even in cases when you decide to make a career change. Now that you understand the importance of planning and goal setting, the next chapter will turn those goals into actionable next steps. We will show you how to create a concrete **Assess** objective based on where you are right now. That objective will serve as a guiding compass for your immediate job search. In three years or five years, you will set a new **Assess** objective to help guide you in taking the next career step based on the plan that you are developing for yourself. Remember: Great, satisfying careers don't happen by chance—they are designed!

There is one other layer to consider as you design your path, and that is determining which industries you are drawn to. This is important because when companies have quite a bit of talent competing for positions, they often like to especially consider people who have industry experience in addition to a solid set of skills. Companies feel as though applicants with previous industry experience bring that added level of value to "hit the ground running" by not having to learn new lingo or the marketplace.

So, for example, if Amy began as a human resources coordinator within the corporate office of a retail chain, she would have her best success, and in most cases a competitive advantage, when looking to obtain future jobs from other retail companies rather than, say, jumping from retail to a pharmaceutical firm. It is for this reason that, when you choose your entry-level position with your three- to five-year goals in mind, you do so in an industry that you are drawn to. Take time to research industries and get a feel for them. There are many websites, like the Vault. com, that provide you with industry-specific information on various industries or fields. Then, search for target positions within that industry and start designing your career path by filling in the blanks on what skills and experience will be necessary for you to obtain so that you will be ready when that promotion or job opportunity presents itself.

Remember that although these steps come before we start the process of working through the A^3 model and start to **Assess**, they will save you heartache and pain in the future. The time spent now is an investment that many people do not make, but if you do, it will keep you moving ahead in achieving personal and professional happiness instead of dealing with the frustration of trial and error in your career. It will also perfectly position you to use the A^3 model and develop your WHY message to employers at every step along the way in your career. Your path to success will make sense, and employers won't have to struggle to see how you got there. It will be plain as day to them.

Bottom Line: The Happiness Factor is a process that you go through to first understand what makes you tick as a person. You then use that information as a compass to guide you to pursue opportunities within your chosen field both now and in the future so that you can build a stable career path.

ASSESS: STARTING WITH YOU

> *Simple Principle:* In a nutshell, before you can begin a job search, send a resume, or talk to an employer, you have to have a good handle on who you are professionally and what you bring to the table that will standout to an employer so that he or she will hire you over three or four other highly qualified people.

We are going to give it to you straight here. **Assess** is the part of the process where it all begins, and this is also the part of the process that *most* people skip almost entirely. In fact, most people are inclined to jump right into the job search or resume writing before assessing what they bring to the table. Talk to them and you get the sense that they think their "experience will speak for itself." If you ask us, that's risky considering how competitive it is out there.

After talking with students and professionals alike, we are convinced that the reason why people skip this step of the process is because they are not sure where to begin. Depending on a few factors, when done correctly the **Assess** experience may feel a bit liberating, like a springtime yard sale after years of clutter. That is to say, if you are seven to ten years into your career and have been stacking skills, experiences, and jobs that go way back, your resume is probably cluttered and two to four pages long—it may be your time to clean house a bit. To really assess what makes you stand out as a candidate for potential employers, you will need to look at everything you have to offer and consider what goes and what stays. For example, it might be time to finally let go of that retail sales job you had while you were in college and focus on all the professional-related experiences during which you developed skills.

Now by contrast, if you are just starting out, the **Assess** experience may feel a little daunting; you may feel as though you do not have much at all to bring to the table. In both cases, we are here to help. The first part of the A^3 model will assist you in assessing who you are professionally, what you want out of a potential job or job search, and what skills you bring to the table. The **Assess** model will not take you all the way back to the inception of choosing a career path, but it will help you by providing an accurate snapshot and skills inventory of the path that you have chosen for yourself so far. By doing this, you accelerate yourself down that path ahead of others and package yourself effectively for success in front of employers. During this process, if you discover that you are not happy with the path that you have chosen, then you will also be able to make an honest evaluation for yourself about whether it is time to make a professional life change now or maybe in the future.

Setting Assess Objectives

The best place for you to start is simply by defining who you are professionally. If you followed along with us as we discussed the Happiness Factor and career goal-setting, then you are off to a great start. The next step is to make that actionable based on where you are today and where you want to go in your job search right now.

You know this intellectually—that is to say, if we were to ask, you could tell us that you are either starting your career, looking to change jobs, reentering the workforce, or just staying competitive. But what we are looking for here is for you to write a short, concrete **Assess** objective that you will use to guide your immediate next steps. Great **Assess** objectives cover three important areas:

- What (transition, grow, expand into a specific field or role)

- Where (field or industry, organization size)

- When (time frame)

The first part is about determining **what** you want to do. If you are starting out, rejoining the workforce, or changing career fields, then you want to *transition* into a particular field or role. If you are already working in the field you want but desire to get to the next level, then you want to *grow*. However, if you are looking to make a lateral move—that is to say, you are satisfied with what you are doing but, for example, want to move into a larger company, then you want to *expand* your experience. It is also important to specify what type of role you want to obtain and what you want to be doing.

Next, you want to identify **where** you want to work. This doesn't mean a specific organization as much as it means focusing on one or two industries to pursue as well as the company size or organization type, such as nonprofit or for-profit, that is the best fit for you culturally.

Finally, you want to ground your objective in a time frame and determine when you would ideally like to get that offer letter. Don't be tempted to say something like yesterday or one month from now. Although you may feel that level of personal urgency, you want to give yourself a very reasonable time frame so that you do not get discouraged and become tempted to chase anything that surfaces (see *Happiness Factor*). A reasonable time frame for many people may be three months for experienced professionals and six months for new college grads and those in transition. Remember, you can use your downtime to pursue new skills, internship opportunities, and professional networking opportunities that will help you make new contacts and demonstrate passion for your field to a potential hiring manager.

Here are some examples of strong objectives:

*To transition from retail sales into customer service (**what**) within three months (**when**) working for a small to midsize company (**where**) offering an office or call center environment so that I can gain more experience in working with and helping customers (**what**).*

*To expand my experience in accounting (**what**) by moving from a midsize company to a smaller company (**where**) within the next six months (**when**) so that I can have more responsibility.*

*To use my social work internship and grow my experience in helping others (**what**) at a large nonprofit organization (**where**) within the next six months (**when**).*

We invite you to take some time to think through your **Assess** objective as the first step in defining who you are professionally. One quick but important note: Your **Assess** objective is just for you. You should not put it or any career goal or objective on your resume. We will talk more about that in the next chapter where we will show you how to use your **Assess** objective to drive your job search.

After you have your objective and you understand who you are and where you want to head, the rest of **Assess** is about helping you understand what skills you bring. It's a cataloging of sorts, and this activity will be easier for some than others. For some people, it is easy to recognize what matters and what should be "tagged" when taking an inventory of their skills. We all know the basics: College degree? Check! Good communication skills? Doesn't everyone seem to have a claim on those? In the smartphone age, many people feel that as long as they can skillfully connect with the outside world on their many devices, then that makes for a good communicator, so check!

We have put together a thinking activity to help you thoroughly **Assess** what you bring to a potential employer that really matters. We call it a "Skills Inventory," and there are four categories:

- **Innate Skills**: Here you will list your natural personality traits, such as being organized or detail-oriented.

- **Formal Education and Certifications**: Next, you will include all formal degrees, licenses, or certifications that you have obtained.

- **Acquired Skills**: These are skills that you have learned over time, such as becoming a strong negotiator or presenter.

- **Industry Experience**: Lastly, you will want to list the fields you have worked in and the level of experience you have. For example, you may have worked in a restaurant for two years and a hotel for one year. That means you have three years of experience in the hospitality industry. Maybe one of those years you were a team leader, so you should indicate that as well.

The idea with this exercise is to get you thinking broadly about what you bring to the table. So don't get too caught up into whether something is an innate skill or an acquired skill. For example, some people are naturally organized people, but it is also possible to discipline yourself to be more organized over time, thereby acquiring that skill.

Remember that you are using this system to help you think about what you bring to the table.

To help you further, we have put together a Skills Inventory worksheet template that you can begin to use.

Assess Skills Inventory

Your Assess Objective

To _____ the field of_____within_____at
(Enter, transition into or grow within)   (Timeframe)

a_____company to_____.
(Small, medium or large)   (Learn about a function, gain broader experience or reduce my current workload)

What You Bring to the Table

Innate Skills (Personality traits: Organized, Creative, Analytical)	
Formal Education (Degrees, Certifications, Licenses)	
Acquired Skills (Learned over time: Project Coordination, Problem Solving, Sales Management)	
Industry Experience (Financial Services, Marketing, Healthcare) and Level of Experience Achieved (Entry, Mid, Senior)	

A good place to begin is by pulling out your current resume to refresh yourself on your past experiences and begin to organize the information across the four Skills Inventory categories. Do not end there, though. Talk to family and friends, professors, coworkers, and other people who know you to get a sense of your innate and acquired skills. Consider asking these types of questions:

- I am trying to get some honest feedback for my own professional development. What natural personality traits do you think that I have that would help me be most successful in my career?

- What skills do you believe I have that may be most valuable in supporting the career path I have chosen?

After you have asked people who have given you this honest feedback, then you will begin to layer that information on top of what you have already been able to gather and start to really build out your Skills Inventory. Let's look at some examples to illustrate how to build a Skills Inventory by introducing you to two professionals we know named Jill and John.

Case Study

Jill

Current Occupation: Real Estate Agent

Jill works in an upper middle-class suburb outside of Philadelphia. She is a self-motivated real estate professional who has been in the industry for fifteen years. Jill has always been entrepreneurial and has established a great rapport with her large customer base. In the 1990s and early 2000s, being a real estate agent was a lucrative career for Jill; however, since the economy went into a recession, Jill has had a difficult time selling homes. Many seemingly good deals have fallen through for various reasons beyond her control. This has led Jill to carefully evaluate her professional options.

She has always had an interest in property management and feels that now is the perfect time to make a change, but she feels that making the transition may be difficult because all her experience is in the real estate industry. Jill has a strong track record and has acquired good skills that she can transfer and apply to a slightly different role in property management. In order to set herself up for success against other people who have built a progressive career in property management, Jill will need to start by taking a thorough inventory of her skills.

Jill has completed her **Assess** objective and Skills Inventory.

Assess Skills Inventory

Your Assess Objective

To transition into the field of property management within the next six months, working for a small to mid-sized company to learn the property management function and gain broader experience.

What You Bring to the Table

Innate Skills (Personality traits: Organized, Creative, Analytical)	• Relationship oriented • Organized • Bilingual (Grew up in a household that spoke fluently in English and Spanish) • Professional • Self-Motivated
Formal Education (Degrees, Certifications, Licenses)	• State Real Estate License • Microsoft Office Specialist Certification
Acquired Skills (Learned over time: Project Coordination, Problem Solving, Sales Management)	• Strong business and financial acumen • Full knowledge of sales, rental and leasing process • Communications skills (Listening, verbal, written) • Ability to prioritize and manage multiple things • Excellent negotiator
Industry Experience (Financial Services, Marketing, Healthcare) and Level of Experience Achieved (Entry, Mid, Senior)	• Mid-level professional with 15 years in the real estate industry • Strong knowledge of Bucks and Montgomery counties

Case Study

John
Current Occupation: Customer Service Team Lead

John grew up in Tempe, Arizona, and currently resides in the Baltimore area. He enjoyed his college experience at Arizona State University and was eager to work full-time. He was always told by family and friends that he was good working with people and decided that customer service may be a good path to take, so he took a job in Baltimore with a midsize accounting firm. After twelve months with the company, his willingness to learn earned him a small promotion to the team lead position. He's been with his organization for two years now. He loves working with people and desires to take that next step and go for a management position.

John's current company requires five years of management experience before he can be promoted, so he is considering interviewing with other organizations that currently have management positions open and that don't require a minimum of five years of experience. He knows he'll have to sell himself as a manager even though he has never been a manager.

John has completed his *Assess* objective and Skills Inventory.

Assess Skills Inventory

Your Assess Objective

To grow within the field of customer service by obtaining a supervisor position within the next three months working for a small to medium sized company where I can learn how to manage a team of people.

What You Bring to the Table

Innate Skills(Personality traits: Organized, Creative, Analytical)	• *Organized* • *Planner* • *Hard worker/excellent work ethic* • *Willingness to learn* • *Honest*
Formal Education(Degrees, Certifications, Licenses)	*Bachelors of Science, Liberal Studies from Arizona State University*
Acquired Skills(Learned over time: Project Coordination, Problem Solving, Sales Management)	*Leadership skills (Member of the Boy Scouts of America since age 7; Currently serves as a community leader for the local counsel division) Problem solver and skilled at conflict management (obtained a high performer status on reviews for these skills over the last two years)*
Industry Experience(Financial Services, Marketing, Healthcare) and Level of Experience Achieved(Entry, Mid, Senior)	*Two years of experience as a customer service team lead in a financial firm*

The **Assess** part of the A^3 Model is a critical step to take before the job search begins. It captures the essence of what is on your resume while adding a greater dimension around what makes you unique as a potential candidate. The Skills Inventory helps you to store that information all in one place. When you take the time to do this exercise, what you have is a great snapshot of yourself as a candidate. Now, you will either like what you see and will be ready to barrel ahead with a job search and align this snapshot with what companies are looking for, or there will be some gaps to fix. If you find that there are gaps, we have included a guide offering you some quick fixes.

	SOLUTION
Too Many Short-term Jobs	Have a positive reason for why you had a short-term job, or a series of jobs. For example, you may have been taking some education classes and needed a flexible schedule.
	If several short-term jobs or gaps appear close together on your resume, think about consolidating where it may make sense.
Laid off/Unemployed	In this economy, employers are more understanding that many individuals have been laid off. However, it is important to shift the focus from being unemployed to what you have been during your unemployment to stay connected and enhance yourself professionally.
	For example you may have taken classes, or have volunteered at a large non-profit organization. You may have been attending professional association meetings and tradeshows. Noting this type of information in a cover letter shows that you are a committed professional and that your skills are still sharp.
	While laid off, you may also consider taking a temporary assignment or a part-time position to keep working. These opportunities can provide current, relevant examples to respond to questions in an interview.
Skill Gaps	To address skills gaps on your resume, seek out opportunities to obtain knowledge and application around these skills.
	Formal training via books, webinars and courses can provide you with great foundational information. Remember that you don't always need to gain this experience in business. Look for opportunities to build and strengthen this skill in everyday life so that you can speak with confidence around your abilities. For example, you can strengthen public speaking skills by contributing to a speech at a community event.
No Experience/Minimum Industry Experience	Internships/volunteer opportunities allow you to acquire needed industry experience and skills.
	Many organizations are willing to bring on individuals at no cost to the organization. In exchange, these opportunities can provide you with valuable insight and references as you get your foot in the door.

Now that you have a clearer picture of who you are, we are ready to dive into the next part of the A³ Model, which will help you develop a game plan for your job search. Once you identify a position that you want to pursue, we will show you how to **Absorb** professional insights that you can use to package who you are into what companies need and want.

Bottom Line: **Assess** is a snapshot of what you bring to the table and ultimately how you define happiness and success. Taking the time to do this early and often in your career perfectly positions you to use the A^3 model and develop your WHY message for employers, giving you a distinct competitive edge.

ABSORB: PROFESSIONAL STRATEGIES AND INSIGHTS

Simple Principle: You can wing it, or you can *bring it*. When searching for positions and creating your job-search tools, you have the option to do what people commonly do or to have a real game plan to succeed. *Absorb* is about the calculated steps you take to prepare yourself to be as competitive as possible and stand out once you have the opportunity to get in front of a hiring manager.

Now we are going to dive into the process of looking for job opportunities and have a little fun in the process. Let's start by visualizing ourselves in a familiar place: at the beginning of your search. We've all been there and felt that feeling of dread—where do I begin? For those of you who are still figuring out what you want to do, you are keenly aware that when you do figure it out, an intensive job search is ahead of you. And if you are in that category, knowing the information we are going to share with you now will put you ahead of the game and save you valuable time.

So you need to start a job search. What do most people do? They:

- Scour job boards like Indeed.com or Careerbuilder and apply to thirty jobs a day with the same cover letter and resume, crossing their fingers and hoping they hear back

- Learn of an opportunity through a friend and send in a resume addressed to "Hiring Manager," hoping that it falls on the right desk

- Pick up a local paper and start cold calling companies that advertise employment opportunities

- Seek out the top three companies they would like to work at and stalk their job boards daily for anything that seems interesting

In addition to these tactics, people are drawn to reading career articles and several long books looking for nuggets on what to do and what not to do. How can you not feel completely overwhelmed by all of this information and the daunting reality of a full-time job search? It's no wonder many people give up after a certain point. It does not have to be so hard! In this section, we are going to get straight to the point. For your part, we will ask you to be honest with yourself and resist the urge to think, "This doesn't apply to me," or "My resume is good as is." Trust us—we see the same mistakes every day. Droves of people apply for positions that they are not qualified for, sending out cover letters that sound like they were written by robots with a thesaurus and resumes that read like novels. Very few people get this job search thing right, so we are excited to share with you what we know, direct from the HR office, so that you are the one that gets it right. For those reasons, we invite you to consider that if you aren't getting offered the job that you want as quickly as you want, then there may be something of real value to you in the next two chapters.

Let's begin by creating an organized approach to job searches as opposed to throwing a bunch of resumes out there to see which one sticks. The truth is that spending weeks sending out resumes for positions that seem interesting or in an effort to cast a wide net will only end up draining you of your valuable job search energy. Instead, we will explore a process for creating a job search game plan.

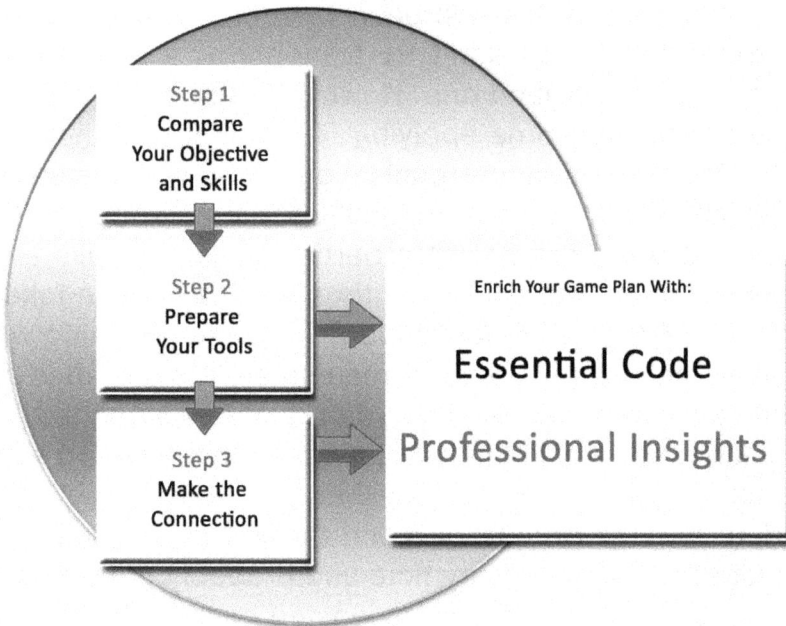

Job Search Game Plan

Step 1
Compare
Your Objective
and Skills

Step 2
Prepare
Your Tools

Step 3
Make the
Connection

Enrich Your Game Plan With:

Essential Code

Professional Insights

Game Plan Step One: Compare Your Objective and Skills

It's no mistake that we begin this process by acknowledging all the hard work that you did in **Assess**. You defined yourself professionally by setting a clear objective and took an inventory of your skills and experience so that you could put together a good snapshot of what you offer. However, all the effort means nothing if you write a fairly generic resume and cover letter and start flinging them out to every job that looks interesting to you. We know that this seems like strange advice. You might feel that it's a numbers game: the more jobs you apply to, the greater chance at getting a call back for an interview. There is a well-known saying that you miss 100 percent of the shots you don't take, and so it's possible that you might take this approach to your job search. You might think that if you don't try to apply to a plethora of jobs, you may never land one. However, trust us; you don't want to spend your time applying to jobs that are not the right fit. There are many organizations that have invested in HR systems that will automatically screen you out of the process if it does not detect a particular set of skills and experience from your resume. In those cases, you've taken your time to prepare an application, yet a human being will most likely never see it. If your resume and cover letter do happen to make it through, and you are phone screened for the position, upon asking a few key questions the recruiter will quickly pick up on the fact that you are not the right candidate and the process will end there. Not only will you have just spent unnecessary time and probably gotten your hopes up, but you may have also wasted the recruiter's time and, should another job arise in the near future with that same company or agency that is a better fit for your skills, you may not be considered a second time.

A much better way is to start your job search process by dusting off that objective you set during the **Assess**. Read your objective and the information you listed on your skills inventory. As you come across a job posting that is of interest to you, ask yourself the following questions:

1. Does this job opportunity enable me to meet my concrete **Assess** objective? Or am I settling?

2. Do I have at least 80 percent of the qualifications and experience that the employer is looking for in the job description? And do I have any of the "nice to haves" that the employer is asking for?

3. Do I have experience in or good knowledge of the industry in which this company sits?

4. Do I know anyone at this company who can help me in this job search process?

Whenever you find job opportunities where you can answer yes to at least the first two questions, then this is a position that is worth pursuing. If you find yourself an opportunity where you can answer yes to all four questions, then you are in excellent shape to be a top candidate for consideration. Let's look at Jill, whom we introduced you to in **Assess**. If you remember, Jill was looking to transition into the world of property management after years in the real estate field. After setting an **Assess** objective and putting together her Skills Inventory, Jill began searching for a job and came across a posting with a company called Pinnacle Properties. When she compared the job posting against her Objective and Skills Inventory, Jill saw that it was a good fit. She had at least 80 percent of the skills and experience that the company was looking for, and the position would meet her goal of transitioning from being a real estate agent to a property manager.

Now, what happens if you can't answer yes to the first two questions? If you come across a job opportunity that seems really exciting or something that you might like to do or think you would be really good at, but you cannot answer yes to at least the first two questions on this list, you should self-select out of applying for the position. Remember that in this competitive environment, employers more often than not have the option of many candidates who are a great fit for the positions that they post. It is next to impossible to compete against other highly qualified candidates if you do not have at least eight out of every ten things that the company is looking for and a few "nice to haves" as well, like added skills or education. Also, if an opportunity falls outside of the objective you have set for yourself, then even if you happened to land the job, you run a great risk of it potentially not working out. If that happens and you decide to leave in a few months, you will have compromised the strength of your resume for the next decade as future employers review your job history. This brings us to the next part of the Game Plan, which involves preparing your tools.

Game Plan Step Two: Preparing Your Tools

Every tool, whether it's a resume, cover letter, or social media page, tells a story—your story. How you prepare these tools and the rules of the game that you choose to follow (or not follow) will play a big role in whether you get noticed and potentially receive a phone call back from a recruiter or hiring manager.

So how do you begin preparing your tools? To start, you must recognize that what you send to recruiters or hiring managers really matters. Same goes for social media pages—the ones that employers are supposed to see, like Linkedin, and even the ones you hope they won't see, like Facebook. The new rule is that if it's out there, it is fair game for hiring managers and recruiters to use in order to get a picture of the type of person you are and thus the type of employee you may be if they were to bring you on board. When was the last time that you Googled yourself? What came up? Would you be happy if a hiring manager or recruiter saw it? Is it consistent with the image that you want to put out there for the world to see? If you answered no to those questions, then time for some quick housecleaning of the social media variety.

Now that you are sure that your social media presence is in check, let's look at some key principles that are important to apply when preparing all your tools. We call them the three Cs:

- Clean

- Concise

- Consistent

Remember that recruiters and hiring managers are very busy people who naturally want to make the candidate review and selection process as easy as possible. It does not mean that they do not want to do a good job; it just means that they are going to gravitate toward the candidate who spells out clearly why someone should hire him or her so they do not have to hunt for the information. Imagine that you are a hiring manager who has a stack of cover letters or resumes that a coordinator placed on your desk for you to review. You can similarly envision someone looking at the same file of applications in a folder that they have created within their e-mail box. Now imagine this individual has about forty cover letters and resumes to choose from. The hiring manager or recruiter needs to make a good decision about how to narrow the field of applicants to a more manageable list of ten people that he or she is going to call for a phone screen. How do you think the decision is made? As these individuals are scanning through the file of applicants, they are going to give each resume a thirty-second glance at most. Within these valuable seconds, they are looking for something to jump out at them that will entice them to increase their review time and either select or discard the cover letter and resume.

The key to getting noticed is to create and send tools that are clean and easy to read. They should include only the best, most important information that is relevant to the hiring organization and in a format that includes plenty of white space. Think about when you took a high school English class and saw that you would be required to read several books throughout the year so that you could write essays. How did you feel when you found out that your assignment required you to read a thick, 300-page book as opposed to a more manageable one that was about 150 pages? It is the same feeling that people who review resumes get when they see a crowded, cluttered resume as opposed to a clean and well-organized one.

Clean

So how can you ensure that you have a clean cover letter and resume? When creating or reviewing these tools, use the following criteria to ensure they are clean and easily noticed by recruiters and hiring managers:

- Aim for 30–40 percent white space

- Choose standard fonts like Arial or Times New Roman

- Use the same font type throughout the document

- Your name may be a larger font but use the same size of eleven- or twelve-point font throughout

- Use bolding and italics very sparingly

- Do not use pictures or more than one type of special character, like bullets

Concise

The next thing to consider when preparing your tools is brevity, which is a necessity for creating clean documents. Creating concise cover letters and resumes are all about incorporating the best of the best material that you have to share with recruiters and hiring managers. One of the biggest mistakes that people make is that they try to cram as much information as possible into long cover letters and resumes, hoping that something of interest will jump out to those reviewing their applications. However, the exact opposite is true when you consider the image of a busy person who is giving each cover letter and resume a quick glance as they move through a large file of potential candidates. If you want to get noticed, it is up to *you* to initially screen out everything but the best information that is most relevant to the position you are applying for and make it very easy for the person reading it to determine why they should continue considering you. Remember, if you are selected for an interview, there will be plenty of time to dive deeper and share more information later on in the process. We cannot stress enough that if you send out cover letters and resumes that resemble literary novels, you seriously run the risk of getting overlooked. Unless you are an executive, there is no reason to have a resume longer than one page.

So how do you create concise documents that will grab an interviewer's attention? You consider 100 percent of the best and most relevant information that you have to share based on the position and what will pique the interest of the recruiter or hiring manager, and then piece it out incrementally. To put it another way, instead of dumping all of your information in a cover letter and resume, you create an approach for sharing it over the course of several potential interactions. Let's identify what those interactions are. When you think about the interview process, there are generally three phases during which you will share your skills, experience, and education with the organization that you hope to work for. That happens first when you send your tools, your cover letter and resume, over for initial consideration. The second step is a phone screen. This is usually a short, thirty-minute call when a recruiter or hiring manager will drill down a bit further and look for reasons to either move you forward in the process or screen you out. The final phase, which may occur over multiple meetings, is the live interview process, when you will be evaluated against a short list of other candidates. The best way to prepare yourself for these three phases is to create a strategy for how you will share information about your professional skills and experiences. Here is an illustration that may help put this concept into context.

Information Sharing Pyramid

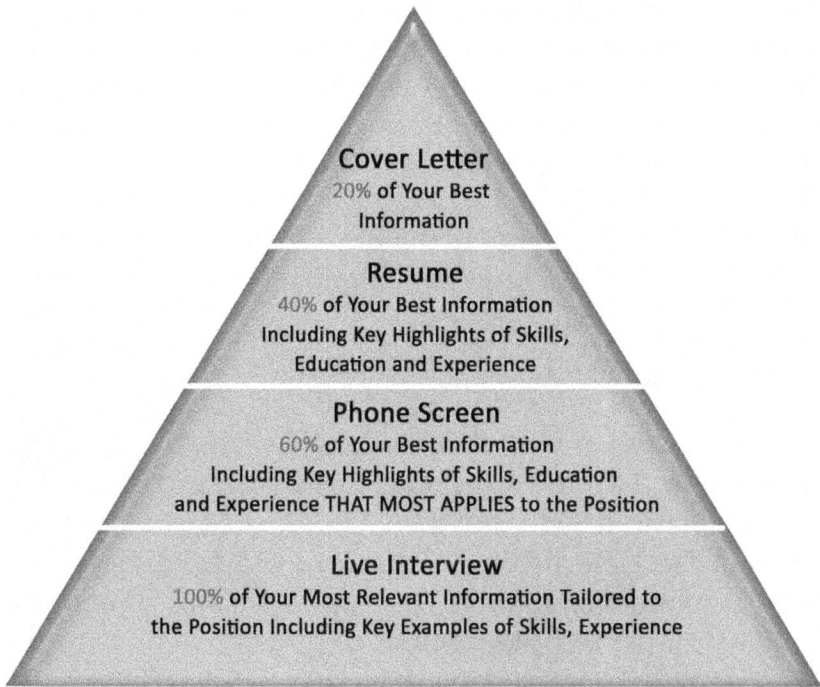

Cover Letter
20% of Your Best
Information

Resume
40% of Your Best Information
Including Key Highlights of Skills,
Education and Experience

Phone Screen
60% of Your Best Information
Including Key Highlights of Skills, Education
and Experience THAT MOST APPLIES to the Position

Live Interview
100% of Your Most Relevant Information Tailored to
the Position Including Key Examples of Skills, Experience

When you have identified a position that you want to apply for, compared your skills and experience against the job posting to determine that you fit at least 80 percent of the qualifications and experience that they are looking for, and feel that the company and position fits well with your **Assess** objective, then you will want to be smart in the way that you reveal information throughout the process of interacting with the company. Think about how product marketers share information with potential buyers. They start with that compelling, thirty-second commercial to get you into the retail store. Once you are happily browsing the aisles, they will often put up a product display or signage that reveals more features and benefits of why you need the product. Of course when you make the purchase decision, take the product home, read the directions and ultimately use it, you are now spending more time with the product, which helps you better grasp the benefits to you as a consumer. Just as it is difficult to get all the information you need about a product from a quick commercial or from a colorful store display, the same principles apply in the way that you should approach how to share information about your skills, experience, and education with potential employers.

Think about the first step of the process from the perspective of a busy recruiter or hiring manager who is hastily reviewing your materials or, before it even gets into human hands, an applicant screening system that is programmed to screen out candidates who do not fit an established profile of keywords. Now, if you already have a standard cover letter and resume that you use, read through it and evaluate the information that you have included. Ask yourself these questions to determine whether you are putting your best "thirty-second commercial" out there so that a recruiter or hiring manager will take notice:

- Does my **cover letter** highlight 20 percent of the *best information* I have to share, such as the two to three key things that I bring to the table?

- Does my cover letter clearly explain the benefits of what I bring as a potential employee to an organization if they hire me?

- Does my **cover letter** specifically say that I am interested in the opportunity and why?

- Does my **resume** only include skills, experience, and education that are professionally relevant to the position I am applying for?

- Does my **resume** include highlights (not paragraphs) of key responsibilities for each position?

- Is my **resume** one page with enough white space?

- Have I removed things from my **resume** that do not qualify as 40 percent of the *best information* that I can share on one page, such as employment objectives, hobbies, or references?

We'll take a look at how Jill transformed her resume as a result of these principles. In her "before" resume, her presentation was not clean, there was too much information, and the resume was two pages. In the "after" resume, you will see how Jill used the space on her resume wisely to provide need-to-know information in a clean and organized way.

Jill Before Resume

Jill A. Cohen
115 School Lane
Telford, Pa 18969
(215) 449-XXXX
JillC15@gmail.com

OBJECTIVE: My objective is to obtain a position in a property management company where I can use my extensive background in the real estate industry to help customers and knowledge of sales and rentals to benefit the organization.

EXPERIENCE:
RE/MAX Reliance, Souderton, Pa
Real Estate Agent Commercial and Residential, 2003-Present
Represented commercial clients and residential customers in the sales process. Developed and implemented individualized marketing strategies to exceed customer expectations. Generated sales of $5MM in 2011 and $6MM+ in 2012, which exceeded average sales for the area. Produced lead flow through creating an incentive program that provided incentives to both the buyer and sellers. Developed relationships with local real estate agents to increase my referral network. Organized local community events in Bucks and Montgomery counties to build awareness and generate lead flow to the area. Negotiated win-win outcomes for all clients with buyers, sellers, local builders and leasing agents.

Coldwell Bank Realty, East Norriton, Pa
Licensed Real Estate Agent and Concierge, 2001-2003
Successfully guided homebuyers and sellers through the sales process and purchase of properties. Generated lists of available properties that were compatible with the buyer's needs and financial resources. Established a good communication flow with other agents, buyers, sellers, loan officers and title agencies involved in the home buying and selling process. Coordinated all appointments for all parties involved by working with both the buyer and seller to agree to mutually convenient times and places. Present during all home inspections and final walk- through. Provided resources to out of town buyers including moving services, local area guides, employment listings and local school information.

Keller Williams Real Estate, Blue Bell, Pa
Licensed Real Estate Agent, 1998-2001
Built relationships with other agents to assist in the purchase and sales of homes. Worked closely with my clients to offer helpful advice and negotiate the best offers for their homes. Effectively showed residential properties to potential buyers. Listened to my clients to determine their needs and work to satisfy those needs. Acted as an intermediary in negotiations between both the buyer and seller. Ensured that all the paperwork was completed accurately and timely prior to the closing.

LICENSURE:
Licensed Real Estate Agent, Pennsylvania

EDUCATION:
Drexel University, Philadelphia, Pa
Real Estate Program, January 1998

Harry S. Truman High School, Levittown, PA
GPA 3.6

CERTIFICATIONS:
Microsoft Office Specialist Certification
June 2003

COMPUTER SKILLS:
Microsoft Word, Microsoft Access, Microsoft Excel
Words typed per minute: 45

AWARDS:
Awarded the RE/MAX Silver Circle Award in 2007 and 2008 for my sales performance

PROFESSIONAL ORGANIZATIONS:
Pennsylvania Association of Realtors, Member

Jill After Resume

Jill A. Cohen
115 School Lane
Telford, Pa 18969
(215) 449-XXXX
JillC15@gmail.com

CORE SKILLS
· Expert Knowledge of the Real Estate Process
· Strong Communication Skills
· Effective Negotiator
· Relationship-oriented

PROFESSIONAL EXPERIENCE

Real Estate Agent—Commercial and Residential Properties
RE/MAX Reliance, Souderton, PA   07/03-Present
Generated $5MM in 2011 and $6MM+ in 2012, exceeding average sales for the area. Awarded the RE/MAX Silver Circle Award in 2007 and 2008 for sales performance. Produced lead flow through creating a sales acceleration program and participated in community events for Bucks and Montgomery counties to build awareness of services, to increase lead flow and expand network. Negotiated win-win outcomes for commercial and residential clients working with local builders and leasing agents.

Real Estate Agent/Concierge
Coldwell Banker Realty, East Norriton, PA   08/01-06/03
Identified available properties that were compatible with clients' needs and financial resources. Built rapport with agents, buyers, sellers, loan officers and title agencies. Provided a high level of service by coordinating client tours, inspections and final paperwork. Worked with long distance buyers l ooking to relocate and linked them to local area guides, moving services and school information.

Real Estate Agent
Keller Williams Real Estate, Blue Bell, PA   02/98-8/01
Worked with clients to determine their needs and negotiated win-win o utcomes for buyers and sellers. Established relationships with other agents to broaden real estate network.

EDUCATION

Real Estate Program   09/97-01/98
Drexel University, Philadelphia, PA

High School Diploma   09/93-05/97
Harry S. Truman High School, Levittown, PA

LICENSE AND CERTIFICATIONS

Real Estate License   01/98-Present
State of Pennsylvania

Microsoft Office Specialist   06/03
Certification

Now, if you are just beginning the process of creating your cover letter and resume, the guidelines around creating clean and concise tools will help you get started. Here are some other things to consider when writing content.

- **Tailor your standard cover letter and resume for each position you apply for.** With more organizations using applicant screening systems than ever before, it is critical for you to mirror the language of the posting without deconstructing the core nature of your skills and experience so that you can increase your chances of getting picked up and forwarded to a live person. During the phone screen and interview, you will continue to tailor how you present your skills and experience to clearly communicate why you are a good fit for what they want.

- **Always remain focused on *what is in it for the employer*.** If you write your cover letter and resume without looking through that lens, it can be problematic and come across as an opinion piece. Employers like it when you can quantify achievements. Show how your experience and skills helped your prior organization succeed.

- **When describing your skills, especially in cover letters, be sure to *show* it instead of say it.** In short, give examples. So instead of saying, "I am very creative," try, "I participated in all aspects of the creative process for my team's award winning promotional program," or, if you are a new graduate, a modified example may be, "I co-lead the creative process for my college's student outreach program, which has significantly increased campus participation year after year."

As you can see from this method of revealing information, once you get to the phone screen phase, you will begin to share more information with the person who will be screening you. This is a good opportunity to dig a bit deeper and give more details through conversation that would not otherwise be practical to share on paper. However, even in this phase you are still striving to be concise in your answers and only reveal about 60 percent more of your best, most compelling information around skills, education, and experience based on what you have determined from the job posting as being relevant for the position that you are interviewing for. It is not until you get to the last phase, the live interviews, that you should share 100 percent of the relevant value that you would bring to the organization. It is during these live interviews that you'll have time to explain your experience and background when asked specific questions by the hiring manager. In the end, before a decision is made, they will look at all the information you have shared at the critical phases in the process and look for consistency and indicators that you are the best choice for the position.

Consistent

This brings us to our last point on how to effectively prepare your tools, and that is to ensure that you are communicating a professional image and consistent message throughout the process. Let's face it, depending on your career choice and industry, the word "professional" may take on very different forms. For example, professional looks very different if you are targeting a bank or prestigious consulting firm as opposed to a career in nursing or perhaps a staff position for an edgy retailer. Regardless of the cultural environment of the organization you are applying for, we can assure you that anyone passing out a paycheck each week is seeking some level of comfort with your professionalism, be it your clean-cut appearance, your ability to communicate verbally and in writing, or on the more liberal end, simply your ability to be reliable and serve the best interest of the business.

Your professionalism and how that is first communicated to a potential employer really matters. There is a reason why recruiters and hiring managers Google you and visit your social media profiles like Facebook and Twitter. They are looking for information contrary to the professional image that you are painting for them in your cover letter and resume. More often than not, they will make a decision to discard your application if they come across photos or rants that are unprofessional. Why? That doesn't seem fair—business is business and personal life is separate! Well, the reality is that it should be that way, but recruiters and hiring managers have their own jobs on the line if they don't make smart (read "safe") hiring decisions. Remember, more often than not you are a complete stranger to them. So think about it: if you were a hiring manager who gets evaluated by a boss on the decisions you make, would you take a risk on hiring a stranger who has compromising information on a public domain when you probably have five other equally qualified candidates who don't? Contrary to what you might think or hope, the rules have not changed. Your image matters—on paper, in person, and online. So be certain that you are projecting the right image at all times, knowing that you are a keyword search away from being evaluated for consistency.

The other area to monitor for consistency is when you modify your cover letter and resume slightly so that they are tailored toward the job you are applying for. This exercise is pivotal, and you should do this, but always consider the possibility that a recruiter or hiring manager may also come across resumes that you have saved to job boards such as CareerBuilder. They will also often search Linkedin to see if you have a profile. You want to be certain that you generally have a consistent message throughout all your visible tools. This should be reasonable if you keep to our advice and only apply for positions where you meet 80 percent of the required qualifications. In these scenarios, the general structure of your cover letter and resume should apply, with the exception of some minor editing around word selection to get picked up by applicant screening systems or catch the eye of a human being who may be scanning through a file.

Game Plan Step Three: Making the Connection

Now that you have your tools fully prepared and a position identified where you will be considered a qualified candidate, the next step is to make the connection. Before you are ready to do that, realize that by virtue of reaching out, you may be called upon shortly for a phone screen or some other informal back and forth, perhaps over email. For that reason, it is critical that you take some time and **Absorb** professional insights that will help set you up for success when you begin interacting with the organization that you potentially want to work for.

So what are professional insights? This is key information that you need to gather on a company and use during a phone screen or interview that will position you as a competent, observant candidate—someone whom the interviewer can imagine fitting right in to the organization. For many hiring managers, finding a candidate who is a good cultural fit is just as important as finding one with the right skills. Professional insights give you those valuable clues into a company's culture and when you use them in conversations with a hiring manager, you begin to stand out. Professional insights are used in two primary ways: through good questions that you will ask the interviewer and through key statements that you will weave into the stories and examples that you share.

Let's talk about what you are looking for and the sources where you can find the information. At a high level, you are looking for any bit of information that gives you a glimpse inside the organization's walls. Like a detective, you are trying to piece together clues that will help you seem as knowledgeable as possible during your phone screen and interview. Why is this important? Because the more you know about them, the more able you are to frame the information you share about yourself in a way that is focused on them.

The first place that you should start is the job posting itself, if you have one. Even if you have heard of this opportunity through a friend or other source, you should be able to search on the company's website to find a posting. Scan the posting for the "message within the message." There are three key areas within a job posting where you can potentially find nuggets of information:

- **First Paragraph or Position Summary**: Frequently, postings will feature an introductory paragraph that sets up the position. Often it talks about the position; however, this summary may also include vital information, such as the department you might be working in and how that department supports the rest of the company. In fact, any organizational information is important to note, such as any notes around growth or expansion. This paragraph may also include details on their "ideal candidate" profile and shed light on the characteristics that matter most to them, such as the ability to multi-task or be a self-starter.

- **Middle of Posting or Skills/Requirements**: While assessing whether or not you meet these requirements, take a second look at what the organization is seeking. Look for things like, "must be flexible" or have a "passion" for something. Hover over words like "changing," "fast-paced," or "collaborative" environment. These things give you a glimpse into what the organization values in its workers.

- **Bottom of Posting or Last Paragraph**: Not every post will conclude with information about the organization, but those that do provide insights. A posting may offer how long the organization has been operating, key values, and its mission. It may be tempting to overlook this information, but remember, you are looking for clues about the organization, and this is rich information. It may not necessarily appear at the bottom of the posting, so you should take note and be observant.

Once you have pulled out professional insights from the job posting, the next step is to use your Internet research skills to identify more information. The first place to start is the organization's website. Start with the "about us" section and, as you did with the job posting, identify information that informs you of the company's values. Do they value creativity and innovation? Do they tout awards and recognition they have received? What is their mission? Where are they heading as an organization? Take note of all these things so that you can use them during an interview and demonstrate the hard work you did to gather this information. It shows that you are interested in the organization, not just trying to get a job.

Next, Google the company and see if there are any articles or blog posts that appear that can provide insight into what the company is doing. For example, a smaller company may have received coverage for sponsoring or participating in a community event, or a larger company may have just opened a new division or expanded into a new country. Blogs are a great way to gain perspective on what the organization shares with the marketplace and what people are saying about the company. Take note of the topics, the jargon, and what image the organization is putting out there. Is their blog edgy, creative, or serious? Figuring this out will give you some insight into the culture or heart of the organization.

The final place to search would be professional networking sites like Linkedin. You can search by company or individual and get a sense of what they are all about. If you have a name of an individual, that is the best case scenario because you can evaluate their profile for insights such as how long they have been with the company, what their background is, and even read recommendations that others have written that may give you clues as to what skills are praised and admired. You can use that information in the interview process to highlight similar skills that you may have. If you are applying for a position that others may already have at the company, such as a customer service representative or a product manager, you may be able to gain some insight into the background of others who work at the organization.

Using Professional Insights

Here is an example of how professional insights work. The following table shows how someone who is highly qualified for a marketing coordinator position and is anticipating the opportunity to interview might prepare themselves for the initial connection by absorbing professional insights. In this case, the candidate is looking at the job posting, company website, blog, and Linkedin. You will see where they are able to get insights and then make notes that they will be able to use when connecting with an employer by highlighting their own examples and stories to align with what the company values.

Job Posting	Posting Says	Professional Insights
Marketing Coordinator	Ability to prioritize and work creatively within deadlines, comfortable with a changing and fast-paced environment	• The company values creativity but also productivity. • Things change quickly, and you need to be comfortable with effortlessly adapting to change.

Company Website	About Us Says	Professional Insights
About Us	Cofounders envisioned a firm where clients could get the experience of a top New York marketing firm but with the personal service and pricing of a boutique company.	• The company likely offers clients high-quality work at a more economical cost. • This may mean overhead/cost of doing business must be controlled and people most likely do multiple jobs.
Company Blog	**Blog Characteristics**	**Professional Insights**
Blog Post	Bold, splashy, and informative. Posts are made frequently by different people/roles within the company.	• The company actively showcases its creativity to the world and utilizes several people to make that happen. • They may value added skills, like the ability to write blog articles or contribute creatively over and above the actual position they are recruiting for.

LinkedIn	Employee Profiles	Professional Insights
Company page and profiles	The profiles for the cofounders of the company show that they have over fifteen years of experience working in top New York City agencies and began this company seven years ago. There are two other coordinators with profiles for this company. One is an advertising coordinator and the other is also a marketing coordinator. They showcase experience, information, and recommendations that speak to their ability to collaborate, be creative, and manage multiple projects with tight deadlines.	• Based on the cofounders' extensive experience in highly structured, New York City marketing firms, they likely bring a good level of professionalism to this company. However, because it is smaller, people may wear several different hats. • The coordinator profiles indicate that the company welcomes creativity and collaboration (as seen with the multiple blog contributors); however, there is still the expectation of managing multiple projects within tight deadlines. That is going to be a trait that the company looks for from an outsider, especially since it also appeared in the job posting.

So to recap what we have discovered so far, the following are likely important to this company:

- Creativity and collaboration, but also productivity and the ability to meet tight deadlines

- Effortlessly adapting to change in the workflow and environment

- Passion and professionalism to give clients the best work, even if that means doing several jobs as needed

- Contributing to the company's creative engine by offering ideas, written pieces, etc.

Imagine that you are the candidate for this position and that you have absorbed these professional insights. Now that you have summarized what you learned, you are positioned to do the following:

- Work this information into your stories and examples. Talk about how you can be creative while also meeting deadlines. Offer examples of ways you have adapted to change.

- Ask insightful questions that demonstrate you know your stuff. For example, "From what I have seen on your website, your team does quality work. How does your marketing team pull together to develop such creative concepts? How do they work together when there are multiple projects with similar deadlines?"

The best thing about uncovering and showcasing professional insights is that the more you work them into your phone screens and interviews, the more insights will be revealed as a result of a great dialogue with the recruiter or hiring manager. Once that happens, you can create a conversation in which everything you say ties back to what the company needs to hear. This puts you in the best position possible to succeed. Using the above example, if you were interviewing for that marketing coordinator position, you could share a professional insight by saying, "I've had the opportunity to review your website and social media pages, and I noticed how original and creative this firm is. I especially liked your blog and have experience blogging for the company that I interned with." Notice how in this example you would be leading with professional insights and then linking each insight to real personal experiences. The examples you share should be based on the time you have on the call or during an interview and based on the questions you are asked.

Next let's go back to Jill, who is seeking out some professional insights on Pinnacle Properties so that she will be prepared if they contact her for a phone screen. Jill has done the following work and has collected these professional insights:

Job Posting	Posting Says	Professional Insights
Property Manager	Join their hardworking team as they continue to grow. They are looking for an entrepreneurial professional to oversee one of their upscale complexes.	• Pinnacle Properties is growing and considers its properties to be upscale. • The company values an entrepreneurial personality/ background.

Company Website	Page Says	Professional Insights
About Us	The professional team at Pinnacle is comprised of the best and the brightest. We focus on providing extraordinary spaces to our residents and pride ourselves on establishing lifelong relationships with our customers—a key reason why the company has experienced double-digit growth in the last five years.	• The company views its people as being as important to its business strategy as its upscale properties. • Pinnacle is relationship-focused and credits its growth in part to its ability to build great relationships with people.

LinkedIn	Employee Profiles	Professional Insights
Company page and profiles	The two managing partners have been in real estate for over twenty years. One of them has a commercial real estate background, whereas the other specialized in residential and development.	▪ Based on the background of the two managing partners, knowledge of real estate is likely valued highly at this company.
	There are three other property managers with profiles. They showcase experience in construction, real estate, and sales/marketing. People have written recommendations based on their ability to manage leasing operations, attract new residents, and provide excellent customer service.	▪ The property manager profiles indicate that sales and customer service go a long way to attracting and retaining customers.

So to recap, the following are likely important to this company:

- Experience in real estate, sales, and marketing

- Entrepreneurship and the ability to support the company in its effort to grow

- Building and maintaining strong relationships with customers

Now that Jill has summarized the professional insights that she has learned, she will be able to do the following:

- Work this information into her stories and examples. She can talk about how her experience as an entrepreneurial real estate agent has enabled her to build strong relationships with customers, many of whom are repeat customers and refer others.

- Ask insightful questions that demonstrate her knowledge. For example, "From what I have seen, the company values entrepreneurship, and its people are an important part of its growth strategy. In what ways do your most successful property managers build relationships with customers?"

Let's take a step back for a moment and clarify that the only person who will be fully aware of all this investigative work is you. You want to use the insights you gain as a means of having relevant conversations during a phone screen or interview. These professional insights will be your "secret sauce" that turns your skills and experience into something that, when combined with the information that you've learned, really sets you apart. You will appear to hiring managers as someone who "gets" their culture and someone who they can envision working with every day. Beyond putting a great cover letter and resume out there, this technique is a critical first step in answering the question, *Why Hire You?* Remember that your resume and cover letter, and even an interview during which you appear professional and capable enough, is not a guarantee that you will stand out from the pack. You have to do the legwork to **Absorb** professional insights that will help you understand the organization and identify what they value in individuals so that you can start to shape yourself into the person they want to hire. Once you have absorbed these professional insights, you are ready for that connection with the organization and to get on with the business of interviewing, which we will discuss in the section called **Articulate**.

What Happens When Nothing Happens?

Before we speed ahead to interviewing, we want to give you a glimpse into why you may be perfectly qualified for a position, have a great resume and cover letter, follow all our steps perfectly, and yet never hear back from the company you applied to. It has happened to all of us, so you are not alone. When this occurs, it is critical to understand what may be going on "behind the company curtain."

Think about a time when you attended a live play or performance. What you see is the presentation. You see the beautiful costumes and sets that make the show what it is, and you admire how it all comes together. What you don't see is the chaos that happens when that curtain closes and production set workers are running around changing out props or fixing broken lights, and the actors are jumping in and out of costumes, fixing their hair, and adjusting makeup. It's very similar in an organization.

What you see is the clean, well-written job posting that appears on the company's website. Behind the organization's curtain, multiple things may be happening. They may have lost a manager suddenly, so they quickly post the job to start generating candidates but then soon discover that the director's former colleague is looking for a new job and would be the perfect fit for the role. Or they may post the position and several weeks later, realize that they have to cut money in their budget and decide to postpone hiring until next quarter. Perhaps the management team decides that they should promote internally and select a candidate in whom they are willing to invest time to develop. All of this is going on behind the scenes, and yet from an outside perspective, you start to question yourself and if what you're doing is working.

You'll have more confidence in yourself if you understand what's really going on. Remember that organizations are busy. If you're laid off or currently not working, and your sole focus is on finding a job, waiting days or weeks or months to hear from an organization seems like forever, doesn't it? Keep in mind that hiring managers have multiple things going on at all times, and so a few passing weeks doesn't seem long at all to them. What can you do? Continue to stay focused. If you can find a part-time job, internship to sharpen your skills, or class to attend, it will help you keep busy to avoid the doldrums of waiting for a response from the company.

Bottom Line: **Absorb** is about having a game plan for the way that you search for jobs and prepare your cover letter, resume, and professional social media profiles. However, you ensure that this process is not all about you by gathering and absorbing professional insights on the companies you are applying to so that during a phone screen or interview, you can work that information into your dialogues. When you do this, hiring managers see you as a potential fit for their organization. Once this preparation work is complete, you are ready to reach out and make the connection with the company.

THE ESSENTIAL CODE

Simple Principle: The Essential Code will give you a glimpse into what is going on in the minds of HR professionals and will point you in the right direction so you don't become "that person." The idea of the *Essential Code* is for you to layer this information onto what we are teaching you through the A³ model so that you stand out for all the right reasons and none of the wrong ones.

Let's take a quick pit stop here before we head into **Articulate**. As you know, we are HR professionals who have many colleagues who have had the pleasure of filling many roles over the years. While writing this book, we reflected on some of our own stories and asked our colleagues to share a few of their own.

While exchanging tales of the good, bad, and indifferent, we soon realized that in some cases, what started out with some laughter eventually turned serious; there are good, well-meaning, and talented people who are either unaware that they might be making some mistakes that will sabotage their job search, or they have been given some very bad advice along the way. So, we are going to share with you a few quick excerpts from the front lines of HR and give you some need-to-know advice that we have turned into a concept called *The Essential Code.*

The Essential Code is a quick read that will give you a glimpse into what HR professionals are thinking and point you in the right direction so you don't become someone who makes well-meaning mistakes. The idea of the *Essential Code* is for you to layer this information onto what we are teaching you through the A^3 model so that you stand out for all the right reasons and none of the wrong ones.

From the Desk of HR	Advice and What To Do
On average, when I post a job, I get about one hundred resumes.	**Advice:** I have a full-time job managing a department of 450 people, and so if I need one assistant manager, I am going to focus on the candidate who has great skills and who can eliminate the guesswork for me by articulating how their skills will meet my business needs. This saves me valuable time and makes me feel good about my hiring decision. **What to Do:** Do and say the right things to eliminate the guesswork for hiring managers. It's all about following the steps in **Absorb** and enriching your game plan with information from this *Essential Code*.

From the Desk of HR	Advice and What To Do
One time I received an e-mail from bigmomma37@emailaddress.com.	**Advice:** You might laugh, but I get e-mails from flirtyblonde27. At times when I call and reach someone's voice mail, I hear hip-hop music blasting in the background. I don't know these folks, so these things create an impression—though not a good one. Remember that I have plenty of other resumes to move on to, and so I'm going with the ones that appear to be serious about getting a job. **What to Do:** You cannot forget the small things when it comes to Preparing Your Tools. It is more common for people to overlook these things than you would think. Open a professional e-mail account, change your voice mail greeting, and watch your online persona. Don't give me a reason to disqualify you. Give me a positive feeling about scheduling you for an interview.

From the Desk of HR	Advice and What To Do
Most people struggle with their resumes. I get resumes that list duties such as "printing reports" or "answering phones." Sometimes I get pink paper and other times crazy fonts.	**Advice:** I know that when you are Preparing Your Tools, you want to get noticed. It is tempting to try to tell someone exactly what you have done in the past, but I don't have time, and I won't read it. I need to see exactly how what you did in the past is a good fit for my needs now. Nothing more, nothing less. **What to Do:** The reality is that there is a formula for what kinds of information and how much information to put into a resume, cover letter, phone screen conversation, and first interview. It's a relatively easy formula; you just have to know it.

From the Desk of HR	Advice and What To Do
I get a lot of resumes from people who are not qualified for the position I have posted.	**Advice:** When you apply for positions that you are not remotely qualified, for it wastes my time and your time. When viewing available jobs, it is very important that you are honest with yourself about whether or not you are truly qualified for the job. You'll save valuable time in the process by not applying to jobs you aren't qualified for. Most job postings are taken directly from the job description and offer critical insight into what the role entails and what the organization is looking for. While you may be able to stretch yourself on some "preferred skills," pay attention to the requirements because if you do not possess them, you are not qualified for the position. **What to Do:** Decode the job posting and then Compare it to Your Objective and Skills. If you are qualified, then prepare your tools. Note that if an organization asks you to apply through their careers website or you found the posting on Monster or Careerbuilder, then you are likely being filtered by a computer system that is looking for keywords and phrases. How do you know what keywords and phrases the computer is looking for? Look at the job posting; they are in there! Incorporating as many of these in your resume and cover letter will help you prevent the computer from putting you in the dreaded rejection folder.

From the Desk of HR	Advice and What To Do
One time I received a resume in an envelope with several tea bags included. A whole variety! When I opened it up, all the tea bags fell on the floor. Sure, everyone in the office got a good laugh, but I was very busy that day, and so the tea bags and resume promptly went into the trash.	**Advice:** I've seen it for myself. Many career resources will steer you in the wrong direction when giving advice on how to get noticed. You can have killer experience and great skills, but it will be difficult for companies to focus on those things if they are annoyed by your job search tactics. This is a mistake that you want to avoid. **What to Do:** When you Make the Connection, you want to follow the directions as stated in the posting. Of most importance, you want to show the hiring manager that you respect his or her time. That means you have assessed yourself and know what you bring to the table. It also means that you are applying to jobs that you are reasonably qualified for. If the application process for the job you want asks that you send a cover letter stating your qualifications along with your resume to an e-mail address, that is precisely what you do. No tea bags required. You want to show a hiring manager that you respect his or her time and the established process.

From the Desk of HR	Advice and What To Do
I once had a promising candidate for a position and placed a call to this person's home to have an initial discussion. The candidate's spouse picked up the phone and proceeded to yell the person's name multiple times until the he picked up the phone. There was a baby crying in the background while I tried to talk with him, and he was clearly distracted. Needless to say, the phone screen was brief and never resulted in an interview.	**Advice:** I wish this was an isolated incident, but it is not. A lot of people must feel compelled to pick up their phone no matter what they are doing. This is not a good idea for the same reason as sending teabags or having sexy pictures of you posted online where I can find them—you need to make a hiring manager comfortable about you. You want to be seen as a professional in every way possible throughout the process. These little things do count. **What to Do:** When you receive a call from an employer, don't pick up unless you're in a quiet place and prepared to talk. Don't pick up in the middle of a noisy restaurant or while your pumping gas. The background noise will annoy the hiring manager and make you looked unprepared. If this happens, it may be impossible to recover. Remember that they are calling to talk about your resume, and you won't be ready to sell yourself if you're distracted. Instead, let it go to voicemail and call back when you have some quiet time.

From the Desk of HR	Advice and What To Do
Quite often I post positions and get many outside qualified candidates. However, if someone I trust puts a resume on my desk and tells me that this person would be a great fit for the position, that resume goes to the top of the pile.	**Advice:** Most people groan at the idea of networking. I get it. And it can be tough if you feel like you don't have a network. Well, you can build one. You can still find a great job without networking, but networking can give you an advantage in hearing about upcoming positions or getting your resume directly on the hiring manager's desk. It helps the hiring manager save time and helps you Make the Connection by getting past the red tape. **What to Do:** We all have people that we interact with daily. Whether that's family members, acquaintances, friends, or maybe even former coworkers. Start by notifying the individuals around you that you are looking for opportunities. Tell them the field and type of position you are interested in. You never know who that individual's brother's wife knows. Speaking of networking, Linkedin has changed the game. If you don't have a Linkedin profile or if it is not complete, fix it. You can use your Skills Inventory to list what you bring to the table. Once you've created your profile, use search methods to find others that you know. You may even be able to view their contacts as well. Your profile is important for when employers search your name online, and they do!

From the Desk of HR	Advice and What To Do
"I didn't get along with my boss." "My working environment was challenging." "I wasn't making enough money." "My company didn't keep up their end of the bargain."	**Advice:** I actually hear these things in interviews. When you finally Make the Connection and get in front of a human being, now is your time to shine! If you remember only one word on how to behave during this time, I want you to remember the word "positive." You should be positive, upbeat, and friendly about *everything*. Don't bash your former employer. If you bash them, you'll bash us once you don't like something, and I don't want to be responsible for bringing in that type of hire. **What to Do:** Have a reasonably positive explanation for leaving your last job or for anything in your past that you feel could be potentially negative. If you were fired, don't offer all the gory details. Say you and the organization parted ways. If you are pressed in an interview, always maintain a positive spin on the situation. Practice your answers in front of a mirror if you have to, because this is a key mistake that many people make.

From the Desk of HR	Advice and What To Do
I had a recent candidate who was waiting for her interview to begin in an open office area and decided it was a good idea to have a personal conversation on her phone. As she talked, the administrative assistant, who was trying to complete an important project for the hiring manager, grew increasingly annoyed. After the interview, the administrative assistant shared with me that she felt this individual would not be a good candidate for the position because she lacked self-awareness. I valued her opinion and decided not to extend a second interview to this candidate.	**Advice:** From the moment you arrive on the organization's property, you need to be interviewing. Your interactions with the security guard, receptionist, and administrative assistant all count. **What to Do:** It's important to begin building a rapport with *everyone* you meet along the way. Assume everyone you meet has ties to the decision makers and could be asked for feedback. Be friendly, positive, upbeat, and self-aware with each person.

From the Desk of HR	Advice and What To Do
A few years back I had an interview with an individual who put on her resume that she was self-employed for a period of about eighteen months. When I inquired about this, she proceeded to talk for twenty minutes about how she had left her current job to start a bakery. She took out a loan with a partner who got pregnant and left her holding the bag for the bakery. She could not manage it alone, it fell apart, and she went bankrupt.	**Advice:** Too much information! When you are interviewing, everything you offer is fair game. I can't tell you how many times candidates get caught up in all kinds of personal details. I don't need to know that you care for your elderly parent at home, that you have three kids, or that you have an upcoming surgery. Don't tell me your sad story about how you got laid off and are about to lose your house or how your attempt at starting your own business failed and so now you need stable work. Where do I get these examples? All real stories from real candidates who never made it to a second interview. Remember, it's not about your personal life, and an interview is not a therapy session. It's about what you bring to help *my* organization be successful. I am giving you a shot to tell me that, so seize the moment or someone else will. **What to Do:** When you get an interview, you are very lucky. Don't bog the hiring manager down with a million details. They should know *nothing* about your personal situation. Hiring managers may try to ask around about questions that might uncover such personal details, however if you stick to safe topics like the weather, sports or local events, then you'll give them nothing to use against you.

Now that you know what not to do during interviews, we are ready to share with you what you can do to be successful and **Articulate** Why Hire You.

Bottom Line: Don't be these people. Stand out for all the right reasons.

ARTICULATE: BUILDING YOUR WHY

Simple Principle: All the work you have done so far has enabled you to define who you are professionally and build a good game plan around what you bring to the table. You also learned how to **Absorb** insights into what is important to the organizations that you apply to *and* the hiring managers who are considering you. Now you are ready for the interview and the chance to **Articulate Why Hire You**.

In its simplest form, we call it *your* WHY. It's how you communicate during an interview so that a hiring manager understands why he or she should hire you. Now, you may think that it's obvious why someone should choose you, especially if you are particularly qualified for a position or if you have done a great job putting your resume together. You may think that because you know someone at a company you are a shoo-in for the position. Too often we see this sort of behavior play itself out in an interview. Candidates will talk around answers to questions without giving the specifics necessary for a hiring manager to visualize them in the new role. Even great candidates often come in displaying a sense that their experience should speak for itself, or they want to jam in as many talking points as possible to ensure that they have covered *something* that they hope will stick with a hiring manager.

This approach is very risky. If you don't come prepared with a strategy for confidently **Articulating** *Why Hire You,* then all the work that you put into **Assessing** who you are professionally, preparing your tools, and **Absorbing** professional insights will be lost. You will not be certain that you stood out from the pack as a clear frontrunner after a hiring manager has seen five other qualified candidates. For you to be successful, it's critical that you are able to continuously answer the *Why Hire You* question throughout the interview. You see, even if a hiring manager does not come right out and ask you directly, subconsciously he or she needs to know that they are making the best selection out of all the possible alternatives. And they need you to serve it up and make it a no brainer decision for them when comparing you to someone else.

Think about it: That is how you shop for things, right? You make a logical comparison, and more often than not you will purchase the one that seems superior to the others. You might also go with the one that has the most "sizzle," because sometimes we do buy things because they look and feel better than the other choices. You see, being able to clearly communicate *Why Hire You* will get you both of those benefits in an interview. We will show you how to do that by telling stories that highlight your skills in action. We will also show you how to leave a great last impression by confidently delivering your unique WHY power statement. When you use these techniques during an interview, you will position yourself in a way so that you stand out from the competition and energize a busy hiring manager who is just looking for someone qualified who can articulate why they should get the job. When you make it that easy, you are creating some excitement and sizzle that makes you look and feel like the right person to select. We want this for you!

Articulate Your WHY

There are many resources that will provide you with the answers to the top twenty-five interview questions or interview tips. However, the challenge is that there are as many interviewing styles and techniques used by hiring managers as there are stars in the sky. There is no way that you can effectively "study" or "cram" for an interview like you would a college exam. You might try, but in doing so the risk is that you go into the interview so laser focused on answers to the questions that you think you may be asked, that you may blank out all together when faced with a question that you do not expect. We know of an HR colleague who asks candidates to choose a dinner that they like to make and walk him through the steps of how they make that dinner. That particular hiring manager loves this technique because people are frequently caught off guard, so he gets to see how they respond under pressure. Also, he evaluates how logical, sequential, and detailed the candidate is in his or her response. He tells us that it gives him a glimpse into how they think, plan, and execute, which are all skills that are critical in most business roles. So let us ask you, how would you respond to an unexpected question like that? We will make it easy for you by showing you how to **Articulate** *your* WHY.

We begin that process by returning to where it all started, with your Skills Inventory. If you remember, the first part of the A^3 model had you **Assessing** who you are professionally, and you did that by putting together a list of your innate skills, formal education, acquired skills, and industry experience. You used this information to prepare your tools, including your resume, cover letters, and, of course, your social media profiles. Once you discovered an opportunity that you were highly qualified for, you made the connection, and in preparation for a callback, you took time to **Absorb** professional insights about the organization using information sources like the job posting or the company website. Now that you are armed with all this information about yourself and the company, you are going to use stories to bring your skills and experience to life in a meaningful way during an interview.

Let's face it, whether it's your close friend or a hiring manager that you just met, people are wired in such a way that we connect and relate to others through stories. So when you are in an interview and a hiring manager asks you a question, you can answer it in one of two ways. You can tell them information by attempting to answer their question, or you can show them what you bring through stories.

We will look at this through an example. You can tell a hiring manager that you are a collaborative person or someone who likes to work with others on a team, which is good information, but this does not allow them to fully understand whether you are really collaborative or someone who likes working with others. If you tell a hiring manager information, they have to take your word for it and draw their own conclusions. However, a better way would involve you showing your skills in action by sharing a story of a recent time when you worked on a large project and proactively asked for feedback from colleagues in other departments so that you could present a proposal that included input from key people in various business departments. This story shows a hiring manager that you are collaborative and enjoy working with others. He or she would hear a story like that and immediately visualize you doing that same thing at his or her company. Now compare that approach against simply telling a hiring manager that you are collaborative and like working with others. Imagine that the same hiring manager heard from three other candidates competing for the same job that they were also collaborative and liked working with others. See how you have an opportunity to use your skills and experience to stand out? To show someone why they should hire you?

Getting Started: WHY Stories

When you develop stories based on your skills and experience, it actually helps you to feel more confident going into an interview because you will be able to easily use this method to answer questions. Stories are also easy to recall, which is especially helpful when you are asked follow-up questions.

Let's talk about how to formulate your WHY Stories. Begin by pulling out your Skills Inventory Sheet and review all the information you included there. Now go back to the job posting for the position that you are interviewing for and highlight what you believe are the top three to five things that the organization is looking for in the candidates that they will be interviewing. Is it project management, being detail-oriented, or working well in a fast-paced environment? Highlight what you think the organization is looking for and see where the match is on your Skills Inventory. You want to ensure that you can connect the dots here.

Now, based on the connection between what the organization wants in this candidate and the skills, education, and experience that you bring, start writing down real-life examples that bring your Skills Inventory to life in a way that will be relevant to the hiring company. You are aiming for at least three to five real-life stories, preferably professional or work related, that paint a picture for the interviewer of those skills in action. That way, they can start to visualize you in that role in their organization. A great professional story has the following characteristics:

- Clear Opening, Middle, and End

- Middle with Specific Details to Illustrate:

    - Problem or Challenge or Opportunity

    - Specifics: Who, What, Why

- Ends on a Business Benefit or Outcome:

    - *As a result we were able to...*

    - *This enabled us to...*

    - *My company benefited by...*

- Can be delivered in two minutes or less

We have put together a planner that you can use to help organize your thoughts when developing these stories.

Articulate Story Planner

Story #1	
	Skills from Inventory Present in this Story:
Story #2	
	Skills from Inventory Present in this Story:
Story #3	
	Skills from Inventory Present in this Story:
Story #4	
	Skills from Inventory Present in this Story:
Story #5	
	Skills from Inventory Present in this Story:

Remember that most hiring managers believe that past behavior indicates future behavior. For that reason, you want to select stories that show how you think and work. Your stories should be specific, and you must be able to easily recall details as many hiring managers will ask follow-up questions to clarify your story. Unless directly asked, steer away from failures, even to say that you learned from them. It is much better to be positive at all times. Here are some examples that will show you what it looks like to bring your skills to life.

Story Example:	Skills from Inventory Present in This Story:
In my current role, I manage the project calendar for our entire department. Three months ago, when we were experiencing our highest volume of projects, I created weekly reports that went out to my manager and all the people who supported the projects that showed who was working on what, who had additional capacity, and what the interdependencies were. This helped my manager know who was available for more work and who was full. It also improved communication among the team.	<ul><li>Project management</li><li>Problem solving</li><li>Works in fast-paced environment</li><li>Proactive</li><li>Team player</li></ul>

Story Example:	Skills from Inventory Present in This Story:
When I was in college, I was very involved in student government. There was a highly charged initiative on campus regarding the development of some open land that would bring in some much needed revenue. There were advantages and disadvantages to both sides, so I organized, secured funding for, and co-moderated a debate that enabled everyone with a point of view to be heard. As a result, the tension subsided a bit, and we were able to see that the students were ultimately in favor of the decision to develop. This enabled us, as their representatives, to vote with confidence in support of the move.	• Leadership • Organization • Diplomatic • Relationship-focused • Budget acumen
Story Example:	**Skills from Inventory Present in This Story:**
When my manager was laid off last year, I was asked to assume some of her responsibilities, including sitting in on some monthly department meetings and communicating new initiatives with my peers. In doing so, I formed a relationship with a manager from another department and asked him to help coach me on the best way to communicate expectations with people who do not report to me. Based on his advice, I scheduled individual meetings with each of my peers to inform them of the department meeting outcomes and get their feedback so that I could be a good representative until a new manager was hired. As a result, the company's needs were met in the interim, and the extra responsibility allowed me to get to know my colleagues even better.	• Collaborative • Relationship-focused • Coachable • Able to lead without authority • Strong communicator

To illustrate this further, let's go back to the example of Jill, the real estate agent looking to transition into property management. One of the best skills that she brings to the table is her ability to negotiate well. This is a skill that she has perfected after years of selling homes, and Jill believes that she can transfer her negotiating skills into a new role as a property manager.

In developing a story to showcase her negotiation skills, Jill can recall a time when she had a client who was moving across the country and could not lower the price of her home without owing money to the bank. Her client could not afford a loss. Jill's client received a fair offer from an interested buyer, but he was not willing to come up in price based on the home's value. Jill was able to satisfy both parties by coming up with a solution that included offering the buyer some of the furniture and wall-mounted TVs in the home if he came up in price. The seller was willing to oblige because it would be less that she had to ship across the country. This was a win–win for both parties involved.

If Jill takes time ahead of the interview to think through the details of this story, she will be prepared to show a hiring manager her negotiation skills in action instead of just saying, "I am a great negotiator." By the way, this story would also demonstrate that Jill is proactive and an effective problem solver. It would leave a great impression. Now let's look at what happens if Jill prepares this story, and she isn't asked about her negotiation skills but rather is thrown a bit of a curveball.

We will flash forward to Jill who is sitting in front of Matt, the hiring manager for Pinnacle Properties. Matt explains a bit about the property manager position and comments on Jill's extensive real estate experience. He then says, "I see you don't have any property management experience. How are you going to effectively work with vendors and suppliers to meet their terms while looking out for our needs?"

Jill now wants to highlight her negotiation skills and will use the WHY Story that she prepared to do just that:

> *Well, Matt, I am a strong negotiator who can manage the interests of multiple parties to create a win–win for everyone involved. In fact, in my current position I recently was involved in a real estate transaction that involved two parties that seemed deadlocked. The seller needed $300,000 for her home in order to walk away from the deal without owing money to the bank. In fact, she needed to move across the country, so time was of the essence. The buyer was only offering $290,000 on the property based on market value. I stepped in and negotiated with the seller to include some of the furniture and wall-mounted TVs in the home in order to help him justify an increase in the offer price. I explained to the seller that the advantage to her is that she would lower her shipping costs and would be able to quickly close the deal so that she could move. Both parties were satisfied. I enjoy negotiating with people to get satisfactory outcomes, and I would use these same skills here to represent our interests and work well with the vendors and suppliers.*

See how easy it was for Jill to talk about her experience and tie it back to Matt's question? She was prepared to talk about negotiation skills, and although Matt asked about working with vendors, Jill knew that she could use the details of the story she created and tailor it in a way to answer his question. She could have used the same example for a whole host of other questions, such as, "Tell me about a time when you had to resolve a challenging situation?" Or, "How do you think outside the box creatively?" Jill's story about the challenging real estate transaction could be tailored to answer both those questions as well.

If you have three to five stories that highlight the skills and experience from your Skills Inventory prepared, you will be all set to answer a range of questions from a hiring manager and help them see why you would be a great fit for the position that you want. What is particularly effective about what Jill did in her example is that she ended the story by linking it to how Pinnacle Properties will benefit. A business benefit or outcome is the only way to end a story because it demonstrates to an employer how your skills will make a difference in their business. Look at the last line:

I enjoy negotiating with people to get satisfactory outcomes, and I would use these same skills here to represent our interests and work well with the vendors and suppliers.

If you end your stories that way in an interview, it will invite the hiring manager to see that he or she can gain these benefits if, and only if, he or she hires you. You are serving it up for them and making it easy for them to see you in this role. As you share these stories, you are staying positive and focused, which builds great momentum throughout the interview. Even if you are asked a downer question, like, "Tell me about your greatest weakness," you should answer that with a positive story that highlights something on the neutral side. For example:

I am very eager to make contributions, so in the past I have volunteered for various committees and task forces that helped drive process improvements within the company. I noticed that time management was becoming a challenge, so I approached my manager for some advice on how to multitask. She helped me prioritize my day, and so I took that as a good learning opportunity.

This answers the question positively and also shows a hiring manager that you are eager, willing, and coachable.

Use every question in an interview to tell a story involving the skills you bring to the table. This will blow the hiring manager away because it will be very refreshing to not have to navigate through the same generic answers that most candidates give. It is unfortunate, but too often hiring managers have to dig, dig, dig until they potentially find something of value in what a candidate is saying, and what they usually find is a bunch of red flags from people who are not prepared. When you bring your Skills Inventory to life in the form of three to five powerful WHY Stories that you adjust to various interview questions, what they'll see from you is an organized, confident, well-spoken candidate who knows exactly what he or she has to offer their organization.

Seal the Deal: WHY Power Statement

Earlier on, we talked about the importance of making a great first impression. We shared with you some tips and techniques in **Absorb** so that you could stand out as you make the connection as well as some examples of what not to do in *The Essential Code.* Now let's assume you are in the interview, and you have been showcasing your skills using WHY Stories. It took a great first impression to get you here, so let's talk about how you make the best last impression. It's called the WHY Power Statement. The WHY Power Statement is short, concise, and hard-hitting; it is what you want the hiring manager to remember about you when you leave. Here is the formula for a WHY Power Statement:

Your Top Attributes + How They Will Directly Benefit the Employer

Remember that throughout the whole interview you have been building the case for Why Hire You with your WHY Stories. Now comes the important part: delivering the WHY Power Statement. So when do you do this? Timing is everything. It is possible that near the end of interview, the hiring manager might ask you a very direct question that prompts your WHY Power Statement. For example:

- Why should I hire you for this position?

- Why are you the best candidate for this role?

However, if the interview draws to a close and you haven't been asked these questions in some form or another, this is exactly when you want to deliver your WHY Power Statement. At the end of the interview, the hiring manager will probably say, "Do you have any questions for me?" Ask what the next step in the interview process is. After the hiring manager answers, sincerely thank him or her for his or her time and then proactively **Articulate** your WHY Power Statement. This will separate you from 99 percent of the other candidates out there. Let's take a look at an example of a WHY Power Statement that may be articulated by someone interviewing for a customer service position. As the interview draws to a close, this individual asks what the next step in the process is. Once the hiring manager responds, it is time to deliver the WHY Power Statement, which might sound like this:

Thank you for your time today. I understand that customer service is one of the highest priorities in this company. My approach is to ask questions and understand customer needs so that I have the information necessary to make the right decision. If you choose me for this role, I will work with each of your customers to resolve concerns and respond in a way that exceeds their expectations. I look forward to that opportunity.

When delivered confidently, a WHY Power Statement like this does a few things. It demonstrates to the hiring manager that you were listening along the way in the interview and that you picked up on some key details. Next, it shows that you are very interested in the position and company. Last, it reassures the hiring manager that your skills and experience will enable you to be immediately successful in the role.

Let's go back to Jill and look at her WHY Power Statement. At the end of her interview, Jill thanks Matt, the hiring manager, for his time and says:

> I've learned a lot about what you are looking for today. If you choose me as your property manager, I will use my real estate knowledge to manage your facility and effectively negotiate with your vendors to secure win-win outcomes. I will also tap into my vast customer network to find new tenants. I look forward to hearing from you soon.

And that is how you seal the deal when closing out an interview to separate yourself from the others you may be competing against.

As you begin to apply what you've learned in this book to your own situation, remember that each part of the A³ model—**Assess, Absorb,** and **Articulate**—builds upon the next and will get you one step closer to being able to clearly answer the question of *Why Hire You.*

Bottom Line: **Articulate** is about developing and delivering WHY Stories so that you can show a hiring manager your skills in action. Preparing these stories will give you confidence in an interview. Closing with a WHY Power Statement will help you seal the deal and separate yourself from 99 percent of all the other candidates out there by leaving a great last impression.

WHY: WHAT'S NEXT

Step 1— Go to www.whyhireyou.com and request your own digital version of the worksheets included in this book, by filling out the Connect Form

Step 2—Complete Your **Skills Inventory**

Step 3—Select a job posting based on your Objective, Skills, Experience, and Education

Step 4—Use the **Job Search Game Plan** to Prepare Your Tools and apply for the position

Step 5—**Absorb Professional Insights** and get prepared before you answer a phone call from a recruiter

Step 6—Remember **The Essential Code** and know the common mistakes people make so you can avoid them

Step 7—Prepare your three to five **WHY Stories** and **Power Statement** and keep those **Professional Insights** handy

Step 8—Confidently **Articulate** *Why Hire You* during an interview. Use your stories to show your skills in action and demonstrate your knowledge of the company by weaving in the **Professional Insights** that you have absorbed into the conversation. Seal the deal at the end with your **WHY Power Statement**.

APPENDIX: EXAMPLE POWER STATEMENTS

EXAMPLE WHY
POWER STATEMENTS

Customer-Focused Professional

Thank you for your time today. I understand that customer service is one of the highest priorities in this company. My approach is to ask questions and understand customer needs so that I have the information necessary to make the right decision. If you choose me for this role, I will work with each of your customers to resolve concerns and respond in a way that exceeds their expectations. I look forward to that opportunity.

Healthcare Professional

This interview has been so informative. I appreciated the chance to talk through my experience as an RN in various healthcare settings, which has helped me really understand the intricate needs of patients. If you choose me for this position, I'll be able to use my experience in patient care plans, treatment, and dealing with concerned family members to make an immediate impact on your team. I look forward to that opportunity.

Technical Expertise Professional

Thank you for all the insight today on how important it is that the candidate you select has deep technical knowledge. In addition to contributing my knowledge of the full lifecycle of software development, should you choose me for this role, I will commit to collaborating with your business partners to fully understand their objectives so that I can not only be a technical resource but an advisor. I look forward to the possibility of continuing this discussion.

Experienced Professional—Broad Industry Experience

I appreciate the time you have given me today to discuss my experience in operations. Working in restaurants, hotels, and retail stores, I've learned best practices around process and procedures that I can bring to this company to support and strengthen what you already have in place. I have also personally sharpened leadership skills that I can use to gain buy-in and support from my new colleagues, so I'm confident that I could be effective starting on day one.

Experienced Professional—Specialized Experience

> *Thank you for the opportunity to talk about my experience in training design, facilitation, and project management today. I believe that having a clear vision and a willingness to collaborate with others has become my personal formula for success. So one of my first priorities in this new role would be to build strong relationships within this department and cross-functionally so that we can harness the best thinking in this company to develop its talent. I'm excited about that possibility.*

College Graduate—No Full-Time Job Experience

> *I appreciate your time today. If you select me for this role, I look forward to the chance to build upon the leadership and communication skills that I learned as part of my summer work and use them to help me be successful here.*

College Graduate—No Full-Time Job Experience

> *Thank you for your time. I am glad we had the chance to discuss my internship during this interview. If you pick me for this position, I will use the planning experience that I learned during the internship and my ability to work well with people to succeed in this position.*